Ilan Eshkeri's *Stardust*

A Film Score Guide

Ian Sapiro

Scarecrow Film Score Guides, No. 15

THE SCARECROW PRESS, INC.
Lanham • Toronto • Plymouth, UK
2013

781.54
E755

Published by Scarecrow Press, Inc.
A wholly owned subsidiary of The Rowman & Littlefield Publishing Group, Inc.
4501 Forbes Boulevard, Suite 200, Lanham, Maryland 20706
www.rowman.com

10 Thornbury Road, Plymouth PL6 7PP, United Kingdom

British Library Cataloguing in Publication Information Available

Library of Congress Cataloging-in-Publication Data
Sapiro, Ian.
  Ilan Eshkeri's Stardust : a film score guide / Ian Sapiro.
     pages ; cm. — (Scarecrow film score guides)
  Includes bibliographical references and index.
  ISBN 978-0-8108-9165-4 (pbk. : alk. paper) — ISBN 978-0-8108-9166-1 (electronic)
1. Eshkeri, Ilan. Stardust. 2. Motion picture music—Analysis and appreciation. I. Title.
ML410.E78437 2013
781.5'42—dc23
                                        2013013193

♾™ The paper used in this publication meets the minimum requirements of American National Standard for Information Sciences—Permanence of Paper for Printed Library Materials, ANSI/NISO Z39.48-1992.

Printed in the United States of America

For Nicki and Jennie

CONTENTS

FIGURES

TABLES

EDITOR'S FOREWORD

Amidst all the many and varied themes that link the different volumes in the Scarecrow Series of Film Score Guides, ultimately the books can be divided into two main categories: volumes on composers who have died, and those on composers who are still living. The Series—and the discipline of film musicology—has benefitted enormously from the opportunity to produce volumes infused with the input of the composer whose score is its subject. With the exception of Janet K. Halfyard's excellent book on Danny Elfman's score for *Batman* (Mr. Elfman did not take up Dr Halfyard's offer to contribute), Gabriel Yared, Ennio Morricone, and Mychael Danna have all been exceptionally generous in their openness towards the authors of their respective volumes. Now Ilan Eshkeri, still a name perhaps less well known to many, has joined their ranks and in many ways complements it too, by being a composer relatively new to the profession and still making his way reputationally and idiomatically.

It is, however, an extraordinary opportunity for the Series to be able to include a volume which looks at this highly contemporary scenario, both compositionally and operationally in terms of the film industry. At the establishment of the Series in 1999, I could not have imagined including either such a relatively lesser known contemporary composer nor a film which, though exceptionally highly rated within the fantasy genre, has not had the universal appeal of others from the genre such as *Lord of the Rings*. It could further be argued that to commission this particular volume was to move away from the original concept of the Series of highlighting benchmark scores and composers. But that would be to ignore how much has changed, both in the Series itself, in the discipline and in the cultural environment. In particular, 'fame,' 'reputation,' 'success' have been utterly redefined in the age of social media and the move away from the movie theater as the principal medium for cinema, and reputation is no longer something which brews steadily over a number of years. Indeed, Dr Sapiro tackles this very issue from the perspective of the studio who were originally unwilling to take a gamble on Eshkeri for the scoring of *Stardust*, despite director Matthew Vaughn's conviction that he was the perfect composer for the job.

This volume therefore sheds light on a number of fascinating aspects of contemporary scoring practice and experience, particularly from the composer's point of view. From the commissioning of the composer to the utterly non-linear fashion in which scores are now temped, written, approved, recorded and edited, we get a composer's-eye view of this process in the creation of the *Stardust* score, a view that blows the dust off a more romantic image of the steady evolution of compositional process that has been sustained for eighty years. In a parallel to Benjamin Winters' volume on Korngold's *The Adventures of Robin Hood*, Dr Sapiro draws on his research to show how a new conceptual model of film-score production is not only appropriate but necessary and, in this case with the benefit of extensive consultation with composers and orchestrators in the British film-music industry, he deconstructs a number of our assumptions about the process. This volume is worth reading for that alone.

Furthermore, one of the ways in which the Series has evolved that is particularly significant to the discipline is the ability to examine change in scoring practice, and how the environment impacts on the composer. In choosing *Stardust* and Ilan Eshkeri to be subjects of this volume, we are considering what they are not, as much as what they are. What better way to examine our preconceptions about score genre and compositional style and their relationship with context than through the eyes and ears of a younger, less experienced composer with a developing reputation, working on a film that had to come out from behind not one but a trilogy of films which dominate its genre. How that emergence is managed by studio, production team, critics and audience is examined in this volume, and it is a fascinating journey with a surprising conclusion.

I am always delighted when the final draft of a new Series volume lands on my desk, but this particular book also brings me great personal satisfaction. I had the privilege of teaching both the subject of the book and its author at the University of Leeds and, as any teacher reading this knows, there is no greater pleasure in education than to see how the small seeds you have contributed to planting go on to grow and blossom. I hope that, as with every book in the Series, you will enjoy the remarkable insights and genuine readability of this companion to a terrific film and its delightfully crafted score.

Dr. Kate Daubney
Series Editor

ACKNOWLEDGMENTS

Stardust
Written by Ilan Eshkeri
Copyright © 2007 Paramount Pictures Corporation d/b/a Paramount
Bella Music
All Rights Administered by Sony/ATV Music Publishing LLC, 8 Music
Square West,
Nashville, TN 37203
International Copyright Secured All Rights Reserved
Reprinted with Permission of Hal Leonard Corporation

Non-linear conceptual model of film-score production in the UK
© 2010 The University of Leeds and Ian Sapiro

I am indebted to a significant number of people, without whose assistance and support this book could not have been written. Firstly sincere thanks must go to Ilan Eshkeri, who not only provided me with a host of materials from the *Stardust* film-score production process, but also records of correspondence between members of the film- and music-production teams, and preliminary sketches and demos created very early in the composition process. He invited me to meet with him at North Pole studios during a very busy period while he was preparing music for another project, and spent an entire day going through the score and recordings for the film, also sitting for interview on further occasions as I delved deeper into the research for this book. Notwithstanding that memories fade over time, and that he has undertaken several projects since *Stardust*, his openness and frankness enabled me to undertake a detailed forensic examination of the score-production process and to understand the collaborative nature of film scoring as he and his colleagues see it. Similarly, his assistance in contacting and encouraging the participation of others involved in the development of the film and its music has been invaluable.

Several members of Eshkeri's music team were interviewed in the course of the research, and thanks are due to Steve McLaughlin, Andy Brown, Robert Elhai, Daryl Kell, and Vic Fraser for their time, information and good humor as I quizzed them about the intricacies of this long-since-completed scoring project. The materials provided by Elhai, Kell, and Fraser supplemented those made available by Eshkeri, notably Elhai's archive of mp3, Finale and Digital Performer files, PDF full scores for cues, and QuickTime videos for cuts of some of the film's scenes. Eshkeri's team, Josine Cohen, Paul Saunderson, and Steve Wright, dealt with my numerous enquiries and requests, and were invaluable in ensuring that I was able to speak with Eshkeri when needed, and that I had access to all of the available materials. Additionally, Julian Kershaw and James Winnifrith both provided valuable contextual information regarding the music production timeline. Owing to scheduling difficulties Matthew Vaughn was unable to speak to me, but thanks must go to his assistant, Leonie Mansfield, for her efforts on my behalf in trying to arrange an interview.

As is often the case in film music, securing copyright clearances to reproduce parts of the score within this book was a time-consuming and often frustrating process, particularly since large studios do not always control the print reproduction rights for their films' scores. Thanks are due to Dan Butler and Hallie Volman at Paramount Pictures, Todd Ellis and Brittany Meredith at Sony/ATV, and Joseph Howard at the Hal Leonard Corporation, who, between them, were able to arrange the necessary permissions.

My series editor, Kate Daubney, has been a constant source of support and guidance, despite some missed deadlines. She encouraged me to undertake the project and has been a source of positivity from proposal to completion. Her faith in my ability has been unflinching and I cannot thank her enough.

Finally I must thank my wife, Nicki, who must have been looking forward to a break from film-music scholarship and proof-reading after I completed my doctoral thesis. Her patience was tested at times, particularly following the birth of our daughter, Jennie, in October 2011, but she has never complained about the time I have had to devote to this book. Whenever I have been stressed she has offered much needed perspective, and this book would not have been finished without her.

INTRODUCTION

Billed with the tagline "the fairy tale that won't behave," *Stardust* is part of an emerging canon of fantasy films that has been growing steadily since the turn of the twenty-first century. Widespread public interest in the genre was spurred by the release of the first installment of Peter Jackson's film adaptation of *The Lord of the Rings* in 2001, which created new production benchmarks for fantasy feature films. Released in consecutive Decembers, Jackson's trilogy won seventeen Academy Awards—in direction, writing (adapted screenplay), film editing, picture, cinematography (twice), visual effects (three times), sound editing (twice), costume, make-up (twice), art direction/set decoration, and original music (score (twice) and song)—and held a further thirteen nominations, effectively establishing *The Lord of the Rings* as the paradigm for the look and sound of the fantasy genre. The significance of Howard Shore's music for *The Fellowship of the Ring* and *The Return of the King*, the opening and closing parts of the trilogy, is highlighted by them being two of very few fantasy film scores to win the Academy Award. That they are the only winners from the genre in the twenty-first century further emphasizes their importance to the sound of the fantasy film in the contemporary industry.

The Lord of the Rings is a double-edged sword, with *Stardust* and all other fantasy films produced since 2001 in both its debt and its shadow. Whereas on the one hand these productions benefit greatly from the way Jackson's films reinvigorated the fantasy genre, they are also unavoidably influenced by the ways in which the trilogy shaped audiences' and studios' perceptions of how such films should look and sound. The challenge for those involved in the production of fantasy films in the twenty-first century is to establish theirs as distinctive and original in itself while also meeting the expectations of fans of the genre. *Stardust* director Matthew Vaughn approached this task by building a production team of trusted individuals who understood and could realize his vision for the film, a team that included composer Ilan Eshkeri.

Though only in his thirties, Eshkeri has been composing scores for film and television for ten years and has been active in the industry for half his life in one capacity or another. He has significant experience of film-score production processes as they exist in both the United Kingdom and in Hollywood, and while his film compositional career has taken place entirely in the post-*Lord of the Rings* era, the majority of his industry training and apprenticeship occurred prior to 2001. Eshkeri is perhaps still approaching his peak in both productivity and quality of output, and since he wrote *Stardust* in the early stages of his career this study provides an opportunity to look at both his development as a film composer and the ways in which industrial processes shape the creative product.

There are very few sources relating to Eshkeri, so the bibliographic information presented in Chapter 1 serves both to introduce him, and to establish the context within which he has developed as a film-score composer. Chapter 2 considers Eshkeri's musical style and approach across his output to date, with a particular focus on aspects of his scoring strategy that feature in *Stardust*. His collaborative partnerships with music producer Steve McLaughlin, contractor/conductor Andy Brown, orchestrator Robert Elhai, and copyist Vic Fraser are also discussed, in addition to Eshkeri's relationship with *Stardust* director Matthew Vaughn. The chapter also considers the place of Take That's song *Rule the World* in the soundtrack and sound world of the film, and appraises the role and value of a hit song and its relationship to a film's score. Neil Gaiman's novel of *Stardust*, Vaughn's film, and the process of adaptation, are the subject of the first part of Chapter 3. This is followed by an evaluation of the place of the film *Stardust* within the fantasy genre, notably with regard to the influential *The Lord of the Rings* series as well as other successful fantasy features such as the *Harry Potter* and *Pirates of the Caribbean* films. Eshkeri's involvement in Vaughn's filmic adaptation, and issues surrounding the musical identity of the film during the production phase are also considered.

Chapters 4 and 5 focus on the music itself, but approach the score from contrasting perspectives. Chapter 4 uses unique primary materials from the film-score production process to undertake a critical evaluation of the creation of Eshkeri's music for *Stardust*. The processes by which the score was created are scrutinized closely through privileged access to computer files including the composer's Digital Performer sketches, the orchestrators' draft and full scores, and MIDI demo recordings, as well as records of and from recording sessions, and documentation relating to the size and constitution of the various recording ensembles. Developments in the score over the three months during which most of the music was composed and realized can be mapped and considered in the context of a new conceptual model of film-score production in the UK. The model provides a framework within which the impacts of practical, political and creative issues on a composer's working methods and approach may be evaluated and understood.

By contrast, Chapter 5 foregrounds the music as heard in the film, analyzing the thematic connections in Eshkeri's leitmotivic score and the ways in which the music relates to narrative and character development. Influences on the music are considered, and along with the analysis this enables the score to be read within the context of a fantasy film score written in the post-*Lord of the Rings* era. Relationships to other films, the influence of their sound-worlds and their composers' approaches, and the expectations of audiences and film-makers regarding what a fantasy film "should" sound like, form the basis of the closing discussion, which highlights the intense demands on a young composer in the contemporary industry.

1

ESHKERI'S MUSICAL AND FILMIC BACKGROUND

Ilan Eshkeri was born in London on 7 April 1977 into a musical family. Encouraged by his parents, he took "formal music lessons on the violin" from the age of four,[1] and he learned the Suzuki method, which he says was "great training for the ear."[2] Eshkeri had a largely classical upbringing—his grandfather played the violin and his mother the piano, and he remembers hearing a lot of Chopin when he was young[3]—but his musical direction changed during his teenage years.[4] It was at this time that he was given a guitar as a present, and he intended to be in a rock and roll band, not an uncommon desire for many teenage boys. However, unlike most adolescents Eshkeri took active steps towards realizing this ambition:

> I was serious about trying to achieve that, so much so that when I was eighteen years old I started asking around friends of parents and stuff, seeing if someone could introduce me to somebody in the industry, and somebody did. Somebody introduced me to a composer called Ed Shearmur.[5]

Shearmur, a protégé of Michael Kamen, was in his late twenties at the time, and just starting his career in film having recently finished a world tour with Robert Plant and Jimmy Page (formerly of Led Zeppelin) on which he had played keyboard and arranged string parts. Eshkeri was "impressed by him and thought the world of him," but any notion he had of following Shearmur into the film business was a distant dream at this stage.[6] He admits that back in 1996, during his gap year before embarking on a degree program in Music and English Literature at the University of Leeds, he did not really know anything about the industry, and the early period of his apprenticeship was spent carrying out menial tasks such as making tea, before he progressed to assisting with the music itself.

Eshkeri began his studies at Leeds in September 1996, where his course included classes in composition, music technology and conducting, alongside those focusing on various periods of literary history and criticism, and, in his final year, a course in the School of English examining the past, present and future of the European film industry. He pursued composition through the first two years of his degree, studying a range of contemporary approaches and techniques with Professor Philip Wilby, but instead of specializing in composition Eshkeri chose to continue his studies in music technology with Professor David Cooper into his final year.[7] Music technology offered him the chance to develop skills in recording and mixing that would complement his composition and broaden his knowledge in a range of musical areas required for film-score composition. Similarly, Eshkeri believes his studies in English Literature now bear directly on his work: the study of narrative relates to the nature of film composition, which helps him read and interpret scripts.[8]

Alongside his degree, Eshkeri developed his knowledge and understanding of the film-music industry and gained valuable professional experience, assisting Shearmur on projects including *Remember Me* (1996) and *The Wings of the Dove* (1997), and spending the University holidays at recording sessions in Abbey Road and the other major London studios. Shearmur also encouraged Eshkeri to gain experience of the processes of film-score composition and production first-hand by writing scores for short films and documentaries; the fact he was already undertaking a significant amount of compositional work may also have led Eshkeri to take the decision to prioritize music technology over composition in the final year of his degree.

Industry Apprenticeship

During the period 1996–2001, Eshkeri met and developed working relationships with a number of significant figures occupying a range of roles in the film-music industry, several of whom he has worked for or with as his career has developed. He recalls his first meeting with music contractor Andy Brown at a recording session for *Remember Me* at Whitfield Street studios:

> I'd never been in a recording studio before. I went into the main room, I didn't even know where the control room was, and I sat by the piano wetting myself. There was an orchestra of about thirty or forty people, it wasn't huge, and Andy—I had no idea [who he was], I'd never met him before—turned around and across this enormous vast room said "excuse me, do you mind hitting an A please on the piano?" And I remember lifting the lid of the piano and thinking "ok, do not mess this up!"[9]

Although he was only Shearmur's intern, Eshkeri joined the players for a drink after the session and became quickly absorbed into the film-musician community. Brown has since become part of Eshkeri's core music team, and the players of the London Metropolitan Orchestra (LMO), for which Brown is the contractor, have recorded all of his film scores to date. He first encountered music producer Steve McLaughlin and copyist Vic Fraser while working on another Shearmur project the following year, *The Wings of the Dove*,[10] and although Eshkeri's involvement with them was negligible at this stage, both have since become part of his core music team. It was also in 1997 that Eshkeri first met Hans Zimmer, who was recording his score for *The Peacemaker* at Air Studios. Eshkeri asked if he could observe the sessions, "and he [Zimmer] said 'yes.' He's a very kind and generous man in that respect, you know. He's very easy going and he's very happy to give people opportunities."[11] Eshkeri also started doing occasional work for Michael Kamen in the late 1990s when, along with James Brett and Michael Price, he was one of

> the three guys in London who worked for well-known composers. There wasn't really anybody else at that time, or very few, and so when people used to come over from America they used to ask for us because we were the only guys who did that stuff. And we kind of ruled the roost in that way. And we would all hang out and have beers together, and we'd pass work to each other so I went and helped out on Kamen projects but, you know, he had his own assistants [Brett and Price] and I was working for Ed.[12]

Eshkeri's relationship with Kamen, which would ultimately prove crucial to his establishment as a film composer in his own right, was forged through a combination of professional and personal connections. He would sometimes help out Brett and Price on Kamen projects, as observed above, and since Shearmur had been trained by Kamen, the two were in regular contact and Eshkeri remembers speaking with Kamen on the phone several times while working for Shearmur.

Eshkeri graduated from the University of Leeds with an upper second class degree in 1999, but just as he reached the point at which he could commit fully to film music, his apprenticeship was abruptly ended by Shearmur's decision to move to Los Angeles, leaving him jobless. He found work as an assistant to punk drummer-turned-music-producer Steve McLaughlin, whom he had first met while working for Shearmur. In addition to broadening his understanding of a range of popular musics, Eshkeri's work with McLaughlin developed his knowledge of and involvement in music production. He also helped McLaughlin to build his North Pole Studios in West London, "literally [buying] the equipment with him and [plugging] it all in," and establishing the roots of a longstanding friendship and working relationship.[13] Alongside this employment, Eshkeri worked with the singer-songwriter Nick Laird-Clowes, formerly of the band The Dream Academy, whose songs had been used in the John Hughes comedies *Ferris Bueller's Day Off* (1986) and *Planes, Trains & Automobiles* (1987), as well as *The Parent Trap* (dir. Nancy Meyers, 1998), and who had co-written lyrics for Pink Floyd's 1994 album *The Division Bell* with friend David Gilmour. Laird-Clowes was "an enormous influence" on Eshkeri, teaching him "everything that wasn't classical music, that wasn't what music 'should' be. [. . .] what it was to be a pop musician or a rock 'n' roller, [. . .] a massive rock 'n' roll education."[14] His time with McLaughlin and Laird-Clowes offered Eshkeri the chance to develop another side of his musical education, their insight as professional popular musicians both complementing and supplementing the academic, generally 'classical' tuition Eshkeri had received at Leeds. In addition to being an experienced songwriter, Laird-Clowes also encouraged him to think about music and sound in different ways, and to utilize the potential of the available technology in his composition. Eshkeri recalls one notable instance of Laird-Clowes's ability to think 'outside the box':

> there were these guys with pneumatic drills outside [the studio] one day and we couldn't record anything, we couldn't do anything, and he [Laird-Clowes] was like "hold on, this is like, it's part of the song" and he ran downstairs with his minidisk recorder and recorded them and tried to put it in the song and I just thought he was a nutcase. And the next day I came in and he'd been working there all night and he'd put in these mad filters [on the sound] and they panned across this thing and suddenly it was part of the song and it was incredible.[15]

Laird-Clowes's integration of sounds more commonly found in a piece of *musique concrete* into his song made a significant impression on Eshkeri, as did his ability to manipulate the sounds using the available studio technology. Eshkeri's avant-garde score for Ralph Fiennes' *Coriolanus* (2012) is "100% a classical score, in that it's all written out, [but] it has a punk-rock edge and energy," demonstrating his ability to synthesize the modern, popular and somewhat radical approaches epitomized by both Laird-Clowes and McLaughlin with the more classical training and knowledge gained through his degree studies.[16] The music includes numerous percussive effects created using instruments ranging from taiko drums to timpani, and less usual items including bits of metal and coiled springs, creating what reviewer Phil Blanckley describes as "an experimental soundscape."[17] Eshkeri's approach was also somewhat experimental. After Fiennes continued to reject the various musical ideas presented by the composer, it became apparent that the director "didn't really want any music at all—or just the bare minimum."[18] This led to Eshkeri moving away from the mainstream and drawing more heavily on the modernist soundworld he had first encountered during his time working with Laird-Clowes. In addition to the percussive effects, the score also features a solo trumpet and a string ensemble created by layering multiple recordings of the composer himself playing violin and cello using unusual techniques. Eshkeri offers significant detail on this process in a promotional video about the film's score:

> I played the [string] instruments either extremely quietly or extremely aggressively. So, for example, on long notes I'd just put the bow on the string [with] no pressure and just brush it across the string just very gently. And I put too much rosin on the bow so you get this kind of "sh," kind of breathy kind of sound as you drag the bow across the string. [. . .] That was one technique and the other technique was to be extremely aggressive and 'dig in' so that you made these really kind of slightly unpleasant, aggressive sounds. And the effect of that would be so extreme that sometimes you'd attack the string so hard that it would bend the string out of tune as you were playing it, and as the bow came off the other end the string would bend back into tune. And these really aggressive techniques on the string instruments made up a lot of the sound of the score.[19]

Phil Blanckley, himself a classical musician, suggests that these ways of working and composing may have been difficult for Eshkeri, noting "I can imagine the challenge this [approach] created for him—when trained in such a classical way, it's often difficult to open yourself up to such a different approach, however he seems to have excelled at the challenge."[20] However, despite its modernism, Eshkeri asserts that the score for *Coriolanus* could have been performed and recorded in a conventional manner with a small string section (some of the sound of which would have been run through guitar amplifiers), solo trumpet, and percussion ensemble,[21] reinforcing his earlier claim that it is "100% a classical score." Additionally, Blanckley's view overlooks the role of McLaughlin and Laird-Clowes in the construction of Eshkeri's musical voice and approach, and his teenage musical tastes which included Nirvana and NWA:[22] he prejudices Eshkeri's formal education at the University of Leeds and effectively ignores the influence of anything not "classical."

This is particularly surprising when it is considered that Eshkeri is not alone in complementing a "classical" musical education with experience of other sounds and styles. Laurence MacDonald observes that Alan Menken studied music at New York University in addition to "[playing] the piano in various nightclubs in Manhattan," and one of Eshkeri's mentors, Mi-

chael Kamen, attended the Juilliard School and that "despite his classical
training, [he] formed the New York Rock and Roll Ensemble."[23] Miguel
Mera reports that Mychael Danna's music degree course at the University
of Toronto "encouraged the study of world music,"[24] and Trevor Jones
followed undergraduate study at the Royal Academy of Music in London
with a postgraduate course at the University of York with the intention of
cultivating his knowledge of a range of contemporary, popular and world
musics. According to Jones,

> The course at York was designed really to fill in gaps in my musical edu-
> cation which the Academy hadn't dealt with: ethnic music, rock, jazz,
> pop, avant-garde, 20th century, electronic, all kinds of music.[25]

Eshkeri's musical style and approach will be considered in detail in Chapter 2, but the diversity of his scores pays tribute to his broad musical
background. Although it may not be as visible as his university education
or his apprenticeships with Shearmur and Kamen, his time with
McLaughlin and Laird-Clowes has played and continues to play an important role in his development as a film composer.

Significant Developments

2001 saw significant developments within both Eshkeri's career and the
film-music industry in broader terms. With limited professional opportunities in London, Eshkeri took the same decision Shearmur had made two
years previously and moved out to Los Angeles to continue his apprenticeship in film music. Once in Los Angeles he approached Hans Zimmer
at his Media Ventures studio (now Remote Control), and, as he had done
in 1997 at Air Studios, Zimmer gave him an opportunity. Eshkeri's connections to Michael Kamen led to Zimmer allowing him to work on *Black
Hawk Down* (dir. Ridley Scott, 2001), even letting him produce some initial
soundscape ideas for the film with a seventy-piece orchestra on Sony's
sound stage, alongside orchestrator/conductor Bruce Fowler. The film
opened in America in December 2001, just one week after *The Lord of the
Rings: The Fellowship of the Ring* received its premiere in the UK.
    Eshkeri was somewhat insulated from the immediate impact of
Shore's *Lord of the Rings* score owing to the nature of his roles while in Los
Angeles. After working on *Black Hawk Down* he joined Shearmur's team in
late 2001 as a production assistant for *The Count of Monte Cristo*, continuing
in his former mentor's employ in the spring of 2002 as an additional programmer on *Reign of Fire*. *The Count of Monte Cristo* is significant because it

marks the first occasion when Eshkeri worked on a single project with all the members of what would become his core team. Alongside McLaughlin, Elhai, Brown, and Fraser, the film's music department also included editor Daryl Kell, who would go on to work with Eshkeri again in this capacity, notably on *Stardust*. These key personnel were also involved in *Reign of Fire*, the final project with which Eshkeri was involved while in America. This is the only fantasy film on which Eshkeri worked while in Los Angeles, but the proximity of the two films' releases—*Reign of Fire* opened on 9 July 2002, seven months after *The Lord of the Rings*—means that the production phase was nearly complete before Peter Jackson's epic was screened in cinemas. Accordingly, Shearmur's score shows little if any influence of Shore's music, though this may also be a result of *Reign of Fire* being set in the near future rather than a distant or romanticized past.

This period in Los Angeles enabled Eshkeri to gain experience on a number of mainstream film projects and continue his professional development. He gained invaluable insight into industrial working practices both in terms of general film-score production in Hollywood, and the specific processes active within Zimmer's studio. He also developed a more detailed understanding of the roles and responsibilities of the various professionals involved in the realization of a film score through his work as part of Shearmur's team. The creative and practical contributions of orchestrators, copyists, conductors, producers, mixers and other music personnel had a profound and sustained effect on Eshkeri. His close working relationships with McLaughlin, Brown, Elhai and Fraser, discussed in greater detail in Chapter 2, form a significant part of his approach to film scoring. However, despite these benefits, after two years in America Eshkeri was no nearer to becoming a composer for film in his own right. Shearmur was now an established composer having emerged fully from Kamen's shadow with the move to Los Angeles, and his relationship with Eshkeri was starting to strain as the latter sought to forge his own career. Accordingly, Eshkeri decided to relocate again, placing distance between himself and his former mentor by returning to the UK in April 2003. He recalls that:

> I preferred my life in London. And like I said, I was young. I was twenty-six, twenty-five even, and I just figured "well I've got time. You know, I could spend a couple of years really trying to make it work in London and if it doesn't work out I can go back [to Los Angeles]." [… But] I really wanted to just see if I could make it by myself.[26]

Eshkeri found work almost immediately on his return to London through a series of fortunate events that had a significant impact on his future career and opportunities.

Early Career in the Post-*Lord of the Rings* Era

In 2003 Kevin Costner approached Basil Poledouris, whose Emmy-award winning score for *Lonesome Dove* (1989) had established his credentials within the Western genre, to write the music for *Open Range*. However, Poledouris did not see the project through to completion—accounts vary as to the reason, ranging from the composer's failing health to his displeasure at seeing a cut of the film temped with music similar to his score for *Starship Troopers*—forcing Costner into a rethink.[27] Since his debut as a producer on *Dances with Wolves* (1990), Costner had worked on individual films with John Barry, Alan Silvestri, Gabriel Yared and Trevor Jones, and had a short collaboration with James Newton Howard in the mid 1990s; given the credentials of each of these composers, Michael Kamen was not a particularly obvious choice.

The selection of Kamen was even more unusual if it is considered that had he never previously scored a Western, and had not actually undertaken a significant film or television project at all since *Band of Brothers* in 2001, a hiatus of nearly two years. Additionally, Eshkeri recalls that Kamen "was already pretty ill by that point"; *Open Range* was the last score that he completed.[28] However, the timing of the project was ideal for Eshkeri, who joined the music team alongside McLaughlin, Fraser and Elhai working in a range of areas of music production, and as an additional orchestrator under the auspices of Elhai and Kamen himself.[29] Working as a full part of the music team alongside these professionals for the first time was significant in cementing their and Eshkeri's working relationships, as well as enhancing his standing as part of the Kamen 'tradition.'[30]

The team flew out to Prague for the project, working with the Prague Philharmonic, and although the schedule was quite intense—Eshkeri says it was hard work and it felt like they did not sleep for days—the whole experience was "brilliant, we had a great time. [. . .] And that's when I started getting closer to Michael."[31] Kamen and Eshkeri did not have long to get to know each other well owing to Kamen's untimely death in November 2003, but when Eshkeri pitched for the opportunity to write the score for a BBC documentary, *Colosseum: Rome's Arena of Death* (later renamed *Colosseum: A Gladiator's Story*, and henceforth referred to simply as *Colosseum* for clarity) in the summer of 2003 he did not hesitate to approach Kamen for a reference. Eshkeri had heard of the project through a friend in the BBC History department, but by the time he was able to submit a demo to director Tilman Remme the production team had already heard a large number of "very interesting samples and some very interesting musical ideas."[32] The BBC's search for a suitable composer had already been in progress for some time—Remme notes that "Ilan was recommended at a very late stage"[33]—and since none of the producers had heard of him, Eshkeri needed a respected industry figure to underwrite him in order to be considered seriously for the commission.

> And Michael Kamen wrote me this amazing letter. I can remember what it said. I said "look can you write me a reference for these guys at the BBC" and he said "yes." And he wrote "to my friends at the BBC. I encourage you to avail yourself of Ilan Eshkeri's talents," something ridiculous, "I applaud his brilliant work." And it was so massively over the top and [so] Michael, but very funny and I guess that helped me get the gig.[34]

For Kamen to have been willing to advocate Eshkeri so strongly, despite having worked with him on very few projects, emphasizes how highly he thought of him. It also bears testament to the quality of Eshkeri's schooling in the Kamen tradition, both through Kamen himself and through his years as assistant to Ed Shearmur, that Kamen was willing to underwrite him in his debut scoring venture. Eshkeri is overly magnanimous in the above quote, however; Kamen's support enabled him to submit some materials for consideration, but it was his qualities as a composer that secured him the contract. Remme recalls that:

> his [Eshkeri's] sample came in and immediately I felt "here is an exceptionally talented young man who can deliver the kind of score that I was looking for." [. . .] As we started talking some [musical] themes started to develop, and it became obvious very, very quickly that he was the man for the job.[35]

Having secured the commission, Eshkeri approached some of Kamen's music team to work on the score, realizing that their experience could help him through the project. He recollects visiting Steve McLaughlin at North Pole Studios, and that although it was only a small project he agreed to help Eshkeri out. *Colosseum* represented what Eshkeri considers "a huge opportunity."[36] There was a generous budget, particularly considering that it was a television film, so he was able to "write big, Wagnerian-style classical music" and approached Andy Brown to contract and conduct a forty-five-piece orchestra.[37] Orchestrations were done by Jeff Toyne and Kamen's orchestrator Robert Elhai, both of whom had previously worked with his former mentor Ed Shearmur, and Eshkeri was able to bring copyist Vic Fraser onto the project meaning that his whole current core music team was involved in his first professional commission as a composer for film and television. The closing credits for *Colosseum* list only Eshkeri, McLaughlin and the London Metropolitan Orchestra from the music team, though Brown, Toyne, Elhai, Fraser and others are credited fully at the end of the mini documentary "*Colosseum: A* Composer's Story," which is included on the DVD release of the film. These credits also include thanks to (among others) Ed Shearmur, Michael Kamen and Nick Laird-Clowes, emphasizing Eshkeri's respect for and appreciation of his various mentors in the industry.

Both Eshkeri and Remme consider the creation of the score for *Colosseum* a collaborative endeavor, though each had very specific roles in the creative process. The director describes Eshkeri as "the inventive genius who has music in his head and who can create music," the composer commenting that Remme was "really inspirational and really forced [him] to excel; very demanding but in a very positive way."[38] As the director, Remme's most active roles in the creation of the score were to evaluate its success at fitting with the film, whether it captured the essence of what he intended for a given scene and worked from an editorial perspective, and guiding the composer in terms of the direction that the music should take. The whole score was recorded on 23 September 2003 at Abbey Road, the culmination of Eshkeri's four months' work on the project.[39] As the credit list for *Colosseum* shows, Eshkeri's early work was strongly influenced by his various apprenticeships, and owing to the nature of the film—a historical documentary—the composer was not especially bound by wide-ranging genre conventions or the expectations of an established fan-base. His ability to synthesize the requirements of the picture, the vision of the director, and his own original musical voice reflects not only his training, but also his potential.

Michael Kamen died on 18 November 2003, just over a month after *Colosseum* was aired on the BBC, but even in his death he created a significant opportunity for Eshkeri. Kamen had been commissioned to provide a score for an animated German film, *Back to Gaya*, but at the time of his death "he had only completed a few sketches of the *Gaya* score [. . .] there was only a small amount of music. The bassoon theme for the Snurks was there, and some sketches of the race in the first act."[40] The task of formulating a way of completing the score fell to McLaughlin, who had been producing Kamen's scores for nearly twenty years, and Chris Brooks, also a music producer on the project. They scoured Kamen's back catalogue for rejected and unused musical ideas to form the bulk of the material, but needed composers who understood the style and sound to create additional music and mould Kamen's materials to fit the images.[41] Eshkeri, as a third-generation composer in the Kamen tradition, was an obvious choice, particularly since he had worked alongside the composer on *Open Range* and had only just completed *Colosseum* with McLaughlin and Elhai, both of whom were already working on *Back to Gaya*. It was a style that Eshkeri knew very well, and his experience assisting a number of different composers over the previous seven years made it relatively simple for him to step into another composer's shoes as this project demanded.

The score highlights a range of features of Kamen's orchestral style, several of which can also be readily found in Eshkeri's scores. The delicacy and care with which Kamen's individual woodwind lines are crafted is indicative of his years as an orchestral oboist, and there is a clear preference for horns rather than trumpets for the presentation of imperial, grandiose melodies. Percussion is often used for effect as much as for rhythmic impetus or energy, with the low strings and piano rather than drums and other percussion instruments often charged with the task of generating the music's momentum. Eshkeri's score for *Stardust* displays a number of these hallmarks of the Kamen tradition, and Kamen's influence is keenly felt in Eshkeri's orchestral scores. *Back to Gaya* (by now renamed *Boo, Zino & the Snurks*) received its premiere in Germany on 18 March 2004, and despite being a fantasy film it is musically distinctive owing to the unique way in which the score was constructed. Neither Kamen nor Eshkeri felt any need to relate the music to Shore's score, and while this may be explained by the fact that *Back to Gaya* is an animated film, which automatically sets it apart from other contemporary fantasy features, it raises important questions about the impact of *The Lord of the Rings* within the film-music industry. While Shore's scores are perceived as paradigmatic by the general film-going public, a status enhanced by his two Academy Awards for Best Original Score, this does not necessarily accurately reflect their influence on contemporary composers. This potential gap between perception and process will be explored in greater detail in Chapter 5, with direct reference to Eshkeri's score to *Stardust*.

Leaving aside *Reign of Fire*, on which he was not directly involved in the composition of the music, *Back to Gaya* is the only fantasy film score on which Eshkeri was actively engaged prior to *Stardust*. Of all of his early work in film music, it can be argued that *Back to Gaya* is most crucial to Eshkeri's establishment in the business and his development as a composer. Although the music he wrote for the film had to be in Kamen's style and fit with the extant and sourced materials, his role as a composer who helped to complete Kamen's last film score would carry great weight in future projects. Significantly, although the liner notes for the soundtrack recording mention five composers who were brought onto the project to assist with the completion of the score—Eshkeri, Andrew Raiher, Brad Warnaar, Rupert Christie and Blake Neely—only Eshkeri is credited with "Additional music," the rest receiving co-credits for "Arrangement."[42]

Layer Cake (2004)

Eshkeri's career continued on its upward trajectory through 2004 with his involvement in Matthew Vaughn's film adaptation of J.J. Connelly's novel, *Layer Cake*. Although technically an independent project, it was part-financed by Sony, who asked Steve McLaughlin to oversee production and management of the film's music. *Layer Cake* was scored by Lisa Gerrard, who had risen to prominence following her co-composition credit for *Gladiator* (2000) alongside Hans Zimmer, but as the deadline approached a decision was taken to bring in an additional composer to help her complete the score. The film's producers, Vaughn, Adam Bohling and David Reid, asked McLaughlin to find a co-composer, but with money extremely short at this late stage of production they needed someone of good quality but minimal expense. Despite his relative inexperience, McLaughlin proposed Eshkeri, citing his work on finishing Kamen's last score and underwriting him personally to emphasise his confidence in the composer's ability to meet the brief. However, Eshkeri's first meeting with Vaughn did not go as planned, as he recalls:

> My first meeting with Vaughn was a disaster. He turned up, it was Matthew Vaughn, the producers David Reid and Adam Bohling, Jon Harris the editor, and there were some other people but I can't even remember who they were. [. . .] And I had this disastrous meeting. I thought only Vaughn was going to turn up so I didn't even have an assistant at the studio, it was just me, and the computer crashed and it was just a total nightmare. [. . .] Later Matthew turned up on his own and then we kind of really got going, but I thought I was going to get the sack; it was terrifying.[43]

Despite this inauspicious start, Vaughn returned alone to see Eshkeri again the following day. Eshkeri "stayed up all night writing this 'Drive to the Boatyard,' and he [Vaughn] heard it and he was like 'that's it, you've nailed it.'"[44] The time from these meetings to recording at Abbey Road was just two weeks, and scheduling commitments meant that Eshkeri and Gerrard never actually met, though he "recorded and arranged strings for some of her cues."[45] The official soundtrack recording is dominated by pre-existing pop music artists such as Kylie Minogue, Duran Duran and Joe Cocker, but also includes cues written by each of Gerrard and Eshkeri, as well as "Drive to the Warehouse" for which they are listed as co-composers, and "Opening" which co-credits Eshkeri and McLaughlin.[46] His work on the film also secured Eshkeri a nomination for "Discovery of the Year" at the prestigious Gent film-music festival in 2004. *Layer Cake* further reinforced Eshkeri's working relationships with McLaughlin,

Brown and Fraser, all of whom were already on the project when he was brought into the setup, and he made an excellent impression on Vaughn. Despite his relative inexperience, the director approached him personally when he set about planning his next directorial venture, *Stardust*, though in the meantime Eshkeri continued to develop his career. He scored several projects for television in addition to films in a range of genres—the thriller *Straightheads* (also known as *Closer*), drama *Strength and Honour*, and horror *Hannibal Rising* (all 2007)—though he did not undertake any work in the fantasy genre in this period.

Beyond the Fairytale

Stardust further enhanced Eshkeri's profile within the industry, the score being nominated for "Best Original Score for a Fantasy/Science Fiction Film" by the International Film Music Critics Association in 2007. The same body also recognized him as "Best New Composer of 2007" for his score to *Stardust*. Although such an award is perhaps ironic considering he had been working in the industry for four years and had already completed three film scores as sole composer prior to that project, it is also a measure of the attention drawn to Eshkeri by his work on Vaughn's picture.[47] Since *Stardust* he has worked with leading directors and producers on a number of film projects, as well as providing music for several prominent television series. He succeeded Anne Dudley as composer for the final series of *Trial and Retribution* (2009), and scored parts of season 8 of the long-running BBC crime drama *Waking the Dead* (2009), working both as sole composer and alongside Scott Shields and Chad Hobson. Eshkeri and Shields also collaborated on the HBO/Sky action drama *Strikeback*, co-composing the music for the first two series (2010–2011) before Eshkeri passed the project on to Shields to score as sole composer in 2012. Other such projects include scores for the television films *Micro Men* (2009) and *Eric & Ernie* (2011), a biopic of the much-loved British comedy duo Eric Morecambe and Ernie Wise. His most recent television score, co-composed with former Razorlight drummer Andy Burrows, is *The Snowman and the Snowdog* (2012), the long-awaited sequel to *The Snowman* (1982). With nearly ten million viewers, this was British television Channel 4's most-watched program over the 2012 Christmas period.[48]

In the film arena Eshkeri's ability to work in a variety of musical styles has resulted in him providing scores for films in a diverse range of genres: romantic comedy *Virgin Territory*, horror *The Disappeared*, and *Telstar*, a biopic of British popular music producer Joe Meek, all followed in 2008, with *The Young Victoria*, a dramatization of the early years of the reign of Queen Victoria, one year later. He was part of the scoring team for Vaughn's *Kick-Ass* (2010), and as further recognition of his continuing rise in the business, he featured in *Variety*'s series "Eye on the Oscars 2011: Music Preview," placing him in illustrious company.[49] In the article, "From the Bard to the Bean without missing a beat," Eshkeri discusses his scores for Ralph Fiennes's directorial debut, the Shakespearean war drama *Coriolanus*, and action comedy *Johnny English Reborn*, starring Rowan Atkinson, though in the event it seems that the former score was too avant-garde and the latter film too comical for either to yield him an Academy Award nomination. He has also completed scores for two films by director Mat Whitecross with Ash front-man Tim Wheeler, *Spike Island* and *Ashes* (both 2012), and is currently working on Fiennes's second film, *The Invisible Woman*, due to be released in 2013.

The last six years have also seen Eshkeri develop his industry profile further, working as score producer on *Adulthood* (2007) and *Sex & Drugs & Rock & Roll* (2009), as well as writing and recording a piece for pianist Lang Lang and the London Metropolitan Orchestra for *A Sony Christmas Carol*, a short film produced by Sony in 2010. He created arrangements for Amon Tobin and the Cinematic Orchestra for a celebratory concert at the Royal Albert Hall marking twenty years of the British independent record label Ninja Tune, and also created string arrangements for Tim Wheeler and Emmy the Great's 2011 album *This is Christmas*, a project which led to him collaborating with both artists on film scores in 2012—*Spike Island* and *Austenland* respectively. In the first part of 2012 Eshkeri was commissioned to compose a symphonic work to accompany an exhibition of photographs by the Korean photographer, AHAE, called *Through My Window*.[50] Eshkeri's response to AHAE's photographs (which number over one million, all taken from the same window over a two-year period) is a twelve-movement tone poem, and while his skill in creating music to match or complement visual images will doubtless have been of immense value during the composition of this work, it is perhaps his most unusual commission to date.

In the early stages of his career the diversity of Eshkeri's scoring projects meant that he was not pigeon-holed as a composer who worked primarily in any particular genre. While a perceived lack of experience in a given genre may have initially made it less likely that studios or directors would select him for their films, as his career has progressed Eshkeri's versatility has become one of his great strengths. His stock continues to rise as he begins his second decade as a film composer, with invitations to speak at master classes and seminars, opportunities to conduct suites of his scores at concerts in the UK and overseas, and work with pop musicians on upcoming albums sitting comfortably alongside new film- and television-scoring projects.

2

ESHKERI'S WORKING METHODS AND APPROACH TO SCORING

> All films are a collaboration: you're fulfilling the vision of the director, that's what you're doing. They're all artistic collaborations.[1]

In their seminal text on film-score composition, *On the Track*, Fred Karlin and Rayburn Wright describe film-making as "a team effort, and the team includes many experts."[2] They go on to identify the director and producer as those within the group who "have the greatest influence on the musical style, tone, and attitude of the film."[3] In addition to being one of the "experts" on the production team, the composer must also lead his own creative collaboration in order to meet the stringent and usually short deadlines imposed on music during the post-production period.

Technological advancements in the late 1990s and into the twenty-first century have had significant impacts on the working methods of film composers. While developments in music and sound technologies, computer software, and equipment have doubtless opened up film scoring to a much broader range of music-makers, and made aspects of the music team's jobs simpler or more efficient, corresponding advances in digital picture editing have brought additional pressures and difficulties. Music editor Dan Carlin Sr. provides an account of the post-production process in the early 1990s, when the moviola was used as standard in the film industry for editing the picture. He relates picture editing to the creation of the music as follows:

> The film or videotape editor [. . .] now assembles the entire picture in script continuity. This initial assembly is called a *first cut*. The producer and director, usually with the editor, will meticulously analyze the first cut. [. . .] When polishing is complete and the production is within proper playing time, [. . .] the picture is considered in *final cut*. At this point the main and end titles can be designed and ordered. A composer

and music editor are called in for a *music spotting session* with the director,
producer, and picture editor.[4]

He continues with a detailed consideration of post-production, affirming
that "no definitive music can be written until after the spotting session."[5]
The indication is that the music team would only begin work on a score
following approval of the final cut by the director; the production of a
"locked picture" signalled that no further changes would be made to the
visual images of the film. Richard Davis considers the delivery of the
locked picture to the composer as the first step in the music production
process,[6] and composer George Fenton observes that as late as the mid
1990s the production team "had to lock the picture, then it was yours [the
composer's]."[7] However, with the advent of digital picture editing the
concept of the locked picture was lost,[8] leaving composers and their
teams in an industry where, as Karlin and Wright state, "if you don't start
working until the film is locked, you will find yourself on the scoring stage
without any music."[9] Although music may still be allotted six to eight
weeks in the overall post-production schedule, multiple and frequent
changes to the picture after the initial spotting session can effectively re-
duce the period in which the composer and his team can usefully work on
a score. Trust and understanding between a composer and his key colleagues has always been extremely important for the successful production of film scores, and this is even more the case with the increased time
pressures and levels of expectation of the contemporary industry.

The nature and level of the various collaborations within a music
team will doubtless vary from composer to composer and potentially
from project to project depending on how well established the relationships are. For Eshkeri, mutual respect across the music team and a sense
of everyone striving towards the achievement of a shared goal are fundamental to his working methods. As the composer, he still retains overall
responsibility for the creation and delivery of a film's score, but rather
than simply leading a team of professionals, each of whom plays a specific
role in the process, the *production* of his film scores is truly an act of creative collaboration. Artistic suggestions are encouraged from a range of
individuals who might otherwise play almost no significant part in the
shaping of a score, and the opinions of his core team—music producer
Steve McLaughlin, contractor and conductor Andy Brown, orchestrator
Robert Elhai and copyist Vic Fraser—are always valued highly. Eshkeri's
experience working at Hans Zimmer's studio in Los Angeles can be seen
as at least partly responsible for his inclusive approach to film scoring,
even though the two compositional processes differ significantly. There is
a highly collaborative environment at Remote Control, and the composer
works closely with professionals who fulfill a wide range of roles within

the score-production process. Zimmer has commented that he "[doesn't] see the recording engineer as being separate from the musicians. [. . .] we're all part of the team," a comment that could easily have been spoken by Eshkeri with regard to his own working methods.[10] Vera John-Steiner suggests that collaborations such as these depend on high levels of trust, respect and shared ambition:

> Creative collaborations take many forms. In some groups or dyads, the cognitive and emotional dynamics reach a certain height, after which the collaboration starts to disintegrate. In others, there is a carefully maintained balance, in which individuals who are committed to each other professionally and personally develop a variety of means to protect their partnership.[11]

The long-standing relationships between the various members of Eshkeri's music team are borne out of working together on a significant number of projects over a period of several years. This has led to the "protection" of their collaborative partnerships that John-Steiner suggests is required for continued success. With these considerations in mind, the first part of this chapter evaluates Eshkeri's approach to film scoring and his musical language, identifying and discussing musical commonalities and similarities across the range of projects on which he has worked, and drawing on aspects of these collaborative relationships. The final part of the chapter focuses more closely on *Stardust* and his partnerships with director Matthew Vaughn and the pop band Take That. The role and function of the film song will also be considered here, particularly with regard to its impact on the film's narrative and musical structures, and the relationship between score and song.

Eshkeri's Approach to Film Scoring

Film composers can often be straightjacketed by the requirements of the projects on which they work. Genre conventions, historical or geographic settings, audience expectations and the whimsy of the director (or other members of the production team) can, at times, leave little room for individuality and creativity. Similarly, the omnipresent specter of the temp track can force even experienced composers to create derivative, impersonal scores that might easily be transplanted wholesale into other, similar pictures.[12] Eshkeri responded philosophically when questioned about his approach to film scoring:

I think every film-music composer is obliged to be a chameleon. You
have to be able to write in a variety of styles, so I hope that some sort of
style follows through, but I don't really think about that stuff. Something that influenced me and that I think is very true, was something
that the composition teacher at Leeds University, Professor Wilby, said
to me once. He said, "you shouldn't worry about having your own style
because there are many composers in the twentieth century who have
been so focused on trying to have an original style and do something
different that they forgot to write music." And I think in a certain way I
agree with him, and I think it's not healthy to worry about stuff like
that.[13]

Such a pragmatic approach is understandable, particularly for someone
who spent his early years in the industry working as an assistant to a number of composers, and whose first composition credits for film (as opposed to television) were for additional music (*Back to Gaya*) and as a co-
composer (*Layer Cake*). However, Eshkeri's perspective, and notably his
claim that a film composer needs to be "a chameleon," echoes sentiments
found in other accounts of and by those in the industry (including in several books in this series). A film score will often include musical codes
that enable it to be associated with a specific genre or style of film, and
may relate not only to the film for which it has been composed, but also
to other music within the soundtrack (songs or pre-existing pieces), and
any music quoted implicitly or explicitly within the score itself. A composer's style arises from a combination of their working methods, approaches, and techniques, but the resulting musical 'voice' is mediated
individually by each project on which they work. Accordingly, a composer
treads a very fine line between maintaining an individual style and being
chastised for their scores all sounding the same. The latter circumstance
can result from a particularly well-received and/or commercially successful score that thereafter overshadows the composer's other previous
scores, leading to them becoming marooned in a particular sound world
that arose initially from the focusing of their musical voice through the
lens of one specific project.

　　In addition to avoiding this problem, young composers in the contemporary industry must also contend with increased public awareness of
film music codes, resulting in greater cultural understanding of what a film
score 'should' sound like. While temp tracks have long resulted in composers using specific styles and sounds to oblige directors and studios,
music featured in theatrical trailers now creates similar difficulties.[14] In
general such material is usually drawn from a combination of other film
scores and specially composed libraries, and in addition to reinforcing
film-music codes, is a very public indication of how the final score might
sound. Eshkeri's diverse range of filmic projects has thus far enabled him

to avoid becoming trapped in a single sound-world, but even considering the pressures on young composers he has been able to establish a unique musical style. The creative input of McLaughlin, Brown, Elhai, and Fraser, as well as directors and potentially others besides, contributes to Eshkeri's individual sound; paradoxically, these collaborative relationships serve to strengthen and develop rather than fragment Eshkeri's style, and make it more readily recognizable. Close analysis of a number of his film scores reveals certain characteristics that appear sufficiently frequently to consider them as indicative of his musical style. Since *Stardust* dates from early within Eshkeri's output, the considerations that follow draw on scores composed over the first ten years of his career (2003–2012) to establish his approach to film scoring and the unifying elements inherent in his film music.

General Approaches

There is no single way to approach a film-scoring project, and much depends on the composer's confidence, experience and mindset. Eshkeri has commented that he likes to "change stuff round a lot, because I believe very strongly that to be original in your creativity it's important to always move the goalposts."[15] He expands on this idea, offering an explanation of how he endeavours to keep his creative practice fresh:

> whenever I pick up a guitar I almost always play a G chord. I don't know why, it's just where my hand goes. If I sit at the piano I generally make the same shapes, and you fall into patterns that you just are comfortable doing. And I notice that with my writing as well; I just start to follow chord progressions that I'm just used to. [. . .] I find that if I want to be creative then I've got to, you know, if I get myself into F♯ major it's like the progressions visually and the muscle memory are not clear to me in the way they are in C or G or whatever, right? Or if you tune your guitar into some wacky tuning and you can't rely on your normal kind of things. That also goes for changing the samples I'm using, changing my set-up, writing in a different room, being in a different place and just changing the process. Do I sit down and write a suite and then try and work that into the film? Do I sit down and try and write a cue? I always change that process as much as possible.[16]

Eshkeri's awareness of his creative practice enables him to reflect upon it and endeavor to continue to change and develop his musical output. This process is clearly of great importance to him—some of the measures he outlines in the above quotation are perhaps a little extreme—but it is a measure of the personal investment he has in each score that he views every commission as an opportunity to reinvent himself to some degree.

As a result of this approach, Eshkeri can be seen to have multiple compositional voices, each subsequent voice drawing on and adding to all previous incarnations as he matures further within the industry. This is not to say that his working methods preclude a return to an earlier compositional voice or approach, or to the revisiting of earlier musical material (which will be considered below). Rather that such a return is not borne out of habit, but is a conscious decision that allows an older state to be revisited with the added benefit of new knowledge and self-reflection gained since the last use of such an approach.

Genres

Eshkeri's diverse musical training through his academic studies and various apprenticeships have brought him to a point where he is equally comfortable working in any number of musical genres. His credit list bears testament to his ability to move effortlessly between classical, contemporary and popular music in order to meet the demands of a given film and director. His avant-garde score for *Coriolanus* was composed in the months immediately before he began work on the orchestral, Hollywood-esque music for *Johnny English Reborn*, both of which contrast sharply with the soundtrack for *Spike Island*, for which Eshkeri worked with Ash front-man Tim Wheeler. Nor is this a new facet of Eshkeri's practice. His first scores for Matthew Vaughn—*Layer Cake* and *Stardust*—could not be more different in terms of the narratives they represent and how they sound, though as will be shown below, there are still connections between them. The influence of contemporary practice is also evident in Eshkeri's use of studio techniques to make subtle changes and developments to the sound of his scores.

Maintaining a close awareness of trends and approaches within popular music is extremely important to Eshkeri. His work with leading popular artists, both within and outside the sphere of film music, is crucial to this and enables him to develop his practice in addition to broadening his musical palette. He has created arrangements for performers including Annie Lennox, David Gilmour, and Coldplay, projects which not only offered Eshkeri the chance to work alongside these established popular musicians, but also to learn about the way in which their music is structured and performed. Additionally, collaborations that involve a crossover of classical and popular approaches, such as for Lennox's concert with the BBC Symphony Orchestra, afford him the opportunity to create music (albeit arrangements rather than compositions) that crosses boundaries and straddles musical genres. He has also written film songs, notably the closing credit song for *The Young Victoria*, "Only You" for Sinéad

O'Connor, "Light the Night" from *The Snowman and the Snowdog* with Andy Burrows, and for *Austenland* (2013) with Emmy the Great, as well as working with Take That on *Stardust*. This broad skillset that Eshkeri has and continues to develop is key to his ability to provide scores for a diverse range of films, and continues to play a vital role in his career going forward.

The *Stardust* score generally occupies a classical, Hollywood-esque sound world, and most of the material is performed by an orchestra with the addition of a wordless female choir. However, there are also elements of contemporary studio and compositional techniques and popular influences inherent in the music, the latter of which will be considered in detail below in conjunction with Eshkeri's collaboration with Take That. The role of contemporary techniques and approaches is, in some respects, the more subtle of the two. They are often revealed by close reading of the score and listening to some tracks on the official soundtrack album as opposed to hearing the cues within their filmic context, where the impact of sound effects may cloud the musical clarity.

Contemporary compositional techniques play a specific role in *Stardust*, generating an aural disturbance within the music owing to their incongruity within the general musical soundworld. Such approaches are utilized principally during moments of intense dramatic tension, notably in 4M34 "Lamia's Inn Part 3", 6M67 "Lamia Rides," and 7M73 "Lamia Locks Doors."[17] Towards the end of 4M34 the score contains numerous dissonances with all instruments and voices in a near rhythmic unison, but the sonic soundscape also includes sweeping sounds that are not included in the printed score (see Figure 2.1, below. This example, like all others in the book, is at concert pitch). However, their inclusion on the official soundtrack album indicates that they are part of the musical make-up of the cue rather than sound effects, which would instead constitute part of the sound design of the scene.

Figure 2.1. Reduction of the orchestral score for bars 50–55 of 4M34

The effect is created by each member of the orchestra playing a rapid ascending scale across the full range of their instrument, with the recording then manipulated in the studio. The blurring of the music/sound boundary emphasizes the way Eshkeri is able to use technology both to enhance his score and blend it with the other elements in the film soundtrack. 4M34 is generally underpinned by a driving bass line, but this is interrupted by rapid ascending patterns that sweep up through the orchestra. Starting as normal chromatic scales, the notation changes from regular noteheads to crossed noteheads alongside the instruction "approx. pitches," as shown in Figure 2.2, below.

Figure 2.2. String parts for bars 13–15 of 4M34

The effect is of the music coming apart at the seams fractionally: the tight coherence of the notated scales fragments as actual pitches give way to approximate. The effect of these techniques may be hard to discern when viewing the film, but other contemporary compositional practices have a greater aural presence. Eshkeri uses microtone clusters to cloud parts of the harmony in several cues. Normally found in the violins, the clusters usually grow from single held pitches, expanding outwards from a fixed point. For the most part these clusters are placed at the end of phrases to accentuate crescendos, the introduction of small variations of tuning having the effect of imbuing the music with additional nervous tension, but the most striking use is at the start of 7M74 "Shining" where it is combined with glissandi, semitone trills and *sul pont.* playing. The scoring at this point also includes unusual playing instructions for the piano and horns, as can be seen in Figure 2.3, below.

The descending string lines clash even before the first violins spread into a quarter-tone cluster, and the multiple descending glissandi, none of which include a definitive pitch as the final destination, intermingle and fight for dominance. The overall effect, amplified by the extended techniques written for piano and horns (and further enhanced by the orchestration, which includes bass flute and a quiet tam-tam roll) is a sense of eeriness and unease that matches the ominous approach of Lamia towards Tristan and Yvaine. A simple descending glissando for the first violins may have yielded a similar effect, especially when placed alongside the corresponding musical lines in the divided second violins. However, the addition of the quartertone cluster introduces a sense that something does not quite fit properly in the aural environment without offering significant clues as to why a listener may have that sense of unease.

Figure 2.3. Reduced orchestration of bars 1–14 of 7M74

Thematicism

Although by no means a feature of all of Eshkeri's scores, the presence of notable themes and motifs is relatively common in his works, especially those written for orchestral forces. Some of these musical markers are closely associated with specific characters, others with atmospheres or narrative actions, though they cannot always be strictly considered as leit-motifs. Arnold Whittall defines leitmotif in its basic form as:

> a theme, or other coherent musical idea, clearly defined so as to retain its identity if modified on subsequent appearances, whose purpose is to represent or symbolize a person, object, place, idea, state of mind, su-pernatural force or any other ingredient in a dramatic work.[18]

Adorno and Eisler argue that film does not allow the "large musical canvas" required for a theme "to take on a structural meaning beyond that of a signpost,"[19] a perspective mirrored by Claudia Gorbman who suggests that "any music [. . .] heard more than once during the course of a film [. . .] repeatedly performed by or associated with characters" is better termed as a "film theme" rather than a leitmotif.[20] In her consideration of similarities between the thematic scores of Wagner and John Williams, Irena Paulus uses the phrase "film leitmotif" to describe similar such material:

> A film leitmotif is rather similar to the pre-Wagnerian leitmotif: most often taken literally from scene to scene, it had the role of sign-post for spectators, quite distant from the role of musical symbol with metaphysical implications found in Wagner's operas.[21]

Since Eshkeri's themes are usually employed as representational devices it is clear that they exhibit some leitmotivic properties. However, these are understandably tempered by the medium in which he works, and the use of representational musical ideas varies in its complexity depending on the requirements of an individual film. His dark, brooding score for *Hannibal Rising* features a number of short, cyclic motifs rather than extended themes, and these are closely identified with the largely negative emotions of fear, anger and vengeance that permeate the story. Although in some respects the character of Hannibal Lecter does develop through the film, these aspects of his personality remain generally constant throughout (albeit that fear is replaced by anger, and then by vengeance as the film progresses). That being the case, there being relatively little change in Eshkeri's motifs from appearance to appearance can be seen as wholly representative of Lecter's attitude and state of mind. Rather than mere signposting, simple repetition actually carries significant symbolism in this instance. Similarly, the main theme to *Johnny English Reborn* is used in multiple cues with no significant development of the material. However, although there is some change in the narrative profile of the film, as a comedy (that is also the sequel to a comedy) it is not intended to challenge or even to provoke a sense of deep understanding in a viewer, so subtle leitmotivic adaptation of the theme could be considered out of place in a film of this type.[22]

Thematicism is a key feature of the *Stardust* score, and the various leitmotifs, melodies and their relationships will be considered in Chapter 5, alongside the filmic elements to which they relate. With regard to the current analysis of the composer's style, it is sufficient to comment that *Stardust* is perhaps the most thematic of Eshkeri's scores to date.

Musical Features

There are a number of central musical ideas that can be found consistently across Eshkeri's film scores. These musical fingerprints transcend genres (both musical and filmic) and operate independently of notions of thematicism. While there are inevitably scores in which some elements do not appear—or at least their presence is not immediately apparent—each of the following musical features plays a prominent role in a suitably high proportion of Eshkeri's scores to be considered a fundamental element of his musical apparatus, a building block on which his music is founded.

Rhythm and Meter

Rhythmic propulsion is perhaps the most widespread musical fingerprint across Eshkeri's filmic output, crossing the boundaries between classical, contemporary and popular scores effortlessly. The opening cue of *Coriolanus* lacks melodic and harmonic content, forcing rhythm and timbre into the foreground. It is based on a simple idea of a continuous quaver rhythm that is spread across the unusual, industrial percussion instruments that make up much of the performing ensemble. Accents abound, sometimes on the beat, sometimes syncopated, but always propelling the music forward with a sense of inevitability. Eshkeri's first cue in *Layer Cake*, co-composed with Steve McLaughlin, is similarly driven inexorably forward by the underlying rhythmic elements of the score. The impetus is generated initially by a pulsing bassline that runs throughout the cue, to which percussion is added to establish and maintain a *moto perpetuo*—the chosen instruments are tambourine, snare drum and finally drum kit, as befits material written in a popular music idiom. There is more harmonic content in the *Layer Cake* cue, but there is still generally an absence of melody. This perhaps owes much to its placement in the film, underscoring the opening monologue delivered in voiceover by XXXX (Daniel Craig), but the effect is that it keeps rhythm reasonably close to the foreground of the sonic texture.

Rhythm is not strictly the domain of the percussion section, however, and several of Eshkeri's scores draw heavily on string instruments to provide rhythmic impetus and propulsion. After a short opening section based around sustained chords, wordless vocal phrases and occasional rhythmic interjections on drums, the first cue of *Centurion* is underpinned by an oscillating phrase first introduced by the low strings before being taken over by the whole string section (see Figure 2.4, below). The main melodic ideas of the cue are presented by the horns, and although the violins join them towards the end of the cue the middle and lower strings continue with the repeated quavers throughout. *Johnny English Reborn* also features rhythmic strings in the central part of the opening cue, though the initial impetus of the music is generated by a drum kit in this instance.

Figure 2.4. Rhythmic string ostinato from the opening cue of *Centurion*[23]

Rhythm is also a key component of the *Stardust* score. However, although each of the above examples focuses on the first cue from the stated film, rhythm is not foregrounded at the very start of *Stardust*. In fact, the ethereal texture at the start of 1M1 "Opening: Through the Wall," created by high strings, winds, piano, harp and glockenspiel, actively works to disrupt any sense of the underlying meter of the music (see Figure 2.5, below). However, by obscuring and disguising the beat Eshkeri uses rhythm as a mask to create the impression that the opening horn melody floats out of time. The use of a musical 'box' in the glockenspiel and the repeated patterns in the piano demonstrate a thorough understanding of the differences between rhythm and meter, which are fundamental to the effect even though they blend into the background at this point. Rhythm does come to the fore in some of the film's musical themes, as will be seen in Chapter 5, but *Stardust* is relatively unusual in Eshkeri's output for its combination of subtlety and forcefulness in the presentation of rhythmic devices in the score.

Harmonic Devices

Two principal elements characterize Eshkeri's scores in this area: ascending, often drawn-out musical lines; and high inverted pedal notes. While neither of these devices is particularly unusual or unique to this composer, both occupy prominent places in a number of Eshkeri's scores and contribute towards the character and sound of his music. Ascending musical lines, usually based on minor scales or the octatonic mode of alternating semitones and tones (or vice-versa), are used melodically and harmonically and in various parts of the texture. The driving string ostinato from the opening of *Centurion* is based on such a pattern (see Figure 2.4, above), and occupies a place mid-way between melody and accompaniment. Starting in the background, it moves smoothly to the forefront of the music before it is overlaid with loud brass melodies, at which point it withdraws and continues repeating in the middle of the texture.

Figure 2.5. Opening bars of 1M1 from *Stardust*

Prominent ascending minor scales can be heard at the top of the texture in the opening cue to *Layer Cake*, and also feature throughout Eshkeri's scores to *Ninja Assassin* and *Johnny English Reborn*. In *Hannibal Rising*, an ascending line based on the octatonic scale can be found in several cues.

Usually played by low cellos, this phrase is often the main source of movement within an otherwise generally static texture, which has the effect of enhancing the passing harmonic dissonances it creates with the fixed bass note. The same technique is employed at various points in *Stardust*, with the tone-semitone octatonic scale often the pitch set of choice.[24] Lines such as these are often placed at the front of the texture in this score, notably in 3M29 "Creating the Inn," where an ascending scale is heard over a range of an octave and a half as the music builds (Figure 2.6a), and in 4M34 where successive five-note minor phrases over static harmonies build to the climax of the movement (Figure 2.6b).

Figure 2.6a. Violins from bars 17–20 of 3M29 from *Stardust*, which feature the ascending tone-semitone octatonic scale.

Figure 2.6b. Strings from bars 23–32 of 4M34 from *Stardust*, showing successive sets of ascending five-note minor scales presented over static harmonies.

As implied by the two cues highlighted above, this device is particularly associated with Lamia and the witches in *Stardust*, as is the use of high inverted pedal tones. The eerie, thin sound of these sustained pitches creates a sense of unease, a property that also renders them eminently suited to prominent use in Eshkeri's scores to *Hannibal Rising* and *Ninja*

Assassin. Inverted pedals are usually accompanied by bass melodies or sustained bass notes in these films, emphasizing the height of the pedal and its ethereal qualities in contrast to the depth and strength of the low pitches. High sustained notes are also utilized in *The Young Victoria* and *Johnny English Reborn*, though the effect is quite different to the previous examples owing to the way the rest of the music is scored beneath the sustained notes. There is often no bass note beneath the held pitch in *The Young Victoria*, meaning the inverted pedal anchors the music without grounding it. The melodic ideas below the pedal become suspended in the middle of the sonic texture, generating more of a sense of contemplation or indecision than menace or malice. In *Johnny English Reborn* the technique is used to build tension, but the nature of the score leads to a sense of anticipation in this case, rather than the dread that may be evoked in *Hannibal Rising* or *Ninja Assassin.*

Pre-Existing Music

Pre-existing music takes various guises within film music. The decision to include pieces of this nature is often taken out of the composer's hands, and although they may impact only very slightly on the composer if they operate diegetically or as independent cues (as is often the case with popular music tracks) this is not always the case. If pre-existing works are to be integrated fully with an original score this can lead to additional considerations for the composer when crafting their own music. Tonality, key, harmonic progressions and rhythm, texture, and orchestration take on added importance when attempting to combine new and pre-existing pieces into a coherent cue, as well as any specific features that characterize a pre-existing work. By contrast, a composer may choose to include references to or quotations from pre-existing works by others or from their own previous scores, particularly since this may help in maintaining an individual's style (thereby satisfying the demands of the director). Such excerpts may be blatant or hidden, and can potentially offer those with greater musical knowledge and awareness additional intertextual meanings in a score that may not be apparent to the lay listener. All of these ways of incorporating pre-existing music will be considered here with regard to Eshkeri's scores, especially since this is a particular feature of *Stardust.*

Integration

Pre-existing music plays a significant role in the soundtrack to *The Young Victoria*, the credit list to which includes works by Handel, Bellini, Purcell, Pärt, Johann Strauss the elder, Schubert, Dvořák and Donizetti. Some of the works by these composers operate as stand-alone pieces within the narrative—a short scene from Bellini's opera *I Puritani* is performed diegetically, for instance—but others are woven into the fabric of the score itself. The production notes for *The Young Victoria* outline the approach to pre-existing music taken by Eshkeri and director Jean-Marc Vallée:

> Vallée and Eshkeri were very keen to have the music be fluid, so that a [pre-existing] source piece can subtly shift and become score, or vice versa, even before the audience realizes it. They felt that this unusual approach to music in a period film would keep the viewer engaged and unsure of where the music was coming from. Often times, a piece of source music is referenced later in the score as an emotional touchstone for the audience, such as the refrain from Schubert's *Swan Song* which can be found hidden in a few moments of the film when Albert is feeling alone or when Victoria is thinking of him but cannot be with him.[25]

Co-producer Denis O'Sullivan goes further, suggesting that Eshkeri's integration of the "Ständchen" (Serenade) from Schubert's *Swan Song* (*Schwanengesang*) within his cue of the same name was pivotal to establishing the roots of Victoria and Albert's relationship in the film.[26] He recalls that:

> One of the first pieces we heard from Ilan was his interpretation of Schubert's *Swan Song*, which plays a key role in the film. Ilan saw how Jean-Marc [Vallée] and [editor] Jill [Bilcock] had structured these two intercutting scenes—one between Victoria and a manipulative Melbourne, the other between lovelorn Albert and his brother—and he just tied these scenes together so beautifully with this one piece of music, it was a revelation.[27]

Eshkeri's cue opens with material based on the introduction to Schubert's song—the underlying D–B♭–Gm–A chord progression is presented with bass notes and moving quaver figurations in a similar manner to the source—but he adds a slow, ascending violin line on the top of the texture that gradually develops into a melody. As the cue progresses there are overtones of Schubert but no further quotations, and the piano gradually gains prominence in anticipation of the appearance of the principal "Ständchen" melody. A similar transition from original to pre-existing music is achieved in the first cue of the film, "Childhood." Eshkeri's score opens with harmonically ambiguous string chords and simple descending scales on the piano before giving way to a short, repeated harp motif. The rhythmic impetus of the guitar is retained as the orchestration thickens and the underlying chord progression gradually becomes that of the introduction to Handel's coronation anthem, *Zadok the Priest*. The characteristic rhythmic drive of the Baroque work is withheld for several bars while the harmony is established, smoothing the transition by blurring the division between new and old material. The recognizable semiquaver string lines are only introduced into the texture as the music builds to a climax in the bars preceding the vocal proclamation "Zadok, the priest" that heralds Victoria's coronation at the end of this opening sequence.

Stardust features two prominent pre-existing works within the score: Dvořák's *Slavonic Dance* Op. 46 No. 6, and the "Galop Infernal" from Offenbach's operetta *Orphée aux Enfers* (*Orpheus in the Underworld*), commonly known as the "Can Can."[28] The *Slavonic Dance* is heard during a scene aboard Captain Shakespeare's pirate ship in which the Captain dances with Yvaine to music that appears to be coming from a wind-up gramophone player. On his Blu-ray commentary, Matthew Vaughn observes that the scene was shot to a different piece of music to that heard in the film, resulting in occasional displacement between some actions and sounds within the scene—he notes that Tristan (Charlie Cox), appears to nod his head out of time with the soundtrack owing to this change, for instance.[29] Vaughn's comment is misleading, however—the scene was shot to the *Slavonic Dance*, but the music was adapted and re-recorded for the final soundtrack, leading to some of the audio-visual asynchronicity. Eshkeri recalls that the decision to use a pre-existing waltz was taken collaboratively, and that Vaughn chose this specific work from a selection of *Slavonic Dances* chosen by the composer.

The scene follows a long pirate montage and is immediately succeeded by dialogue between Tristan and Yvaine as the camera pans round and they dance. Both the preceding and following sections of score are original cues by Eshkeri, and some alterations were required to the *Slavonic Dance* to enable the music to run continuously through the scene; accordingly it was not possible to use an existing recording.[30] Bars 1–42 of cue 5M45C "Waltz" match the original *Slavonic Dance*, but have been transposed down a tone from D to C major, matching the closing tonality of the preceding cue, 5M45A "Pirate Montage." A small adaptation in bar 42 marks a divergence from the original—a semitone resolution is replaced by a tone—and the cue continues (now only a semitone lower than the source) for two bars before the soundtrack merges seamlessly into bar 3 of 5M54B "Pirate Waltz" via a perfect cadence from C♯[7] to F♯m. Julian Kershaw's orchestration of the cue is based on Dvořák's scoring of the original piece, though Kershaw often thickens the texture, keeping it more closely aligned with that found in other parts of the *Stardust* score. To an extent, this also masks the fact that the music is a piece of pre-existing repertoire.

By contrast, the "Can Can" is a stand-alone cue, 5M50, and in addition to being recognizable as pre-existing by a larger proportion of the audience, it is not disguised in the ways that the *Slavonic Dance* is. It is heard during a scene on Shakespeare's ship that cuts between a battle between Septimus's men and the pirates, Septimus seeking out Shakespeare, and the Captain prancing around in front of the full-length mirrors in his large, secret dressing room. At the start of the scene the music is shown to be diegetic, emanating specifically from a gramophone player in the Captain's quarters. However, the likelihood of the music being heard on deck is extremely slim, since it would call the Captain's lifestyle into question and damage his reputation (something that is very important to him, as emphasized several times in the film). Fluctuations in the dynamic level initially reinforce the nature of the track as source music, since it is higher in shots of the inside of the boat than in those of the conflict on deck, but this evens out as the music and scene progress, and the music assumes a non-diegetic role. There is some close synchronization between the music and sound effects of sword fighting, and at the end of the track the sounds of broken glass and breathing as Septimus jumps through a window into the water to escape also align closely with rhythmic aspects of the music.

Eshkeri recalls that picture editor Jon Harris first played the "Can Can" against the scene, and the match was well-received by the whole production team. However, as music editor Daryl Kell explains, "later, after the picture had been tweaked and developed, the actual recording that was used started to get a little bit out of sync with the picture, and in this case we just had to re-record that piece rather than using the pre-recorded piece."[31] The resulting cue, 5M50 "Can Can," is more than a simple re-recording, however, and has been cut and spliced together to account not only for the pacing and cross-cutting within the scene, but also for the few lines of dialogue between Shakespeare and Septimus that occur mid-scene. Additionally, the cue is based principally on the popular music-hall version of the "Can Can," which contains some marked differences to the "Galop Infernal" in Offenbach's operetta, principally in the structure of the introduction and the entire closing section. The cue is in the same key as the stand-alone "Can Can," and much of the orchestration is similar, though parts have been fleshed out by Kershaw in line with the rest of the *Stardust* score. Owing to the need to match the visual images, several sections are heard without the usual repeats and there is an uncharacteristic return to material based on the introduction, thinning the texture and dropping the dynamic level significantly to underscore the exchange between the Captain and the prince. This is followed by an abrupt cut to the popular finale, bringing the scene and piece to a conclusion.

Eshkeri's ability to integrate pre-existing music into his scores bears testament both to his apprenticeship in film, notably his experience on *Back to Gaya*, for which he was required to integrate the existing Kamen material with original music in an appropriate style, and his varied musical training. His extensive knowledge of a broad range of repertoires is also significant for his use of quotation and allusion within his film scores.

Quotation and Allusion

Quotation and allusion both refer to the use of pre-existing material in a new context—a cue or a score—but they are defined in markedly different ways in the film-music and general-music literature. In order to discuss this aspect of Eshkeri's film-scoring technique, a brief overview of these definitions is required so as to disambiguate the terms and establish the context in which they are employed in this discussion.

In *Hearing Film*, Anahid Kassabian defines quotation as "the importing of a song or musical text, in part or in whole, into a film's score."[32] She argues that quotation is particularly a feature of compiled scores, defined by Jeff Smith as those which present "a series of self-contained musical numbers, usually prerecorded songs, which were substituted for the repeated and varied occurrences of a score's theme."[33] Kassabian's reference to Smith and the examples she offers within her discussion emphasize her perspective that quotation is a film-music device associated principally with popular music. This view is reinforced by Smith's comment that "the compilation score attained its importance as a commercially self-aware alternative to the neo-Romantic orchestral scores of Hollywood's 'Golden Age,'" and, by extension, all 'classical' orchestral scores.[34] Quotation is defined differently in a purely musical context, however; J. Peter Burkholder's entry in *Grove Music Online* states that it is "the incorporation of a relatively brief segment of existing music in another work," and it is in this context that quotation in Eshkeri's scores is considered.[35]

Allusion is seen by Kassabian as a form of quotation, whereas Burkholder suggests that "some writers consider quotation a type of allusion."[36] That difference notwithstanding, the authors' definitions of allusion are compatible, the former proposing that it is "a quotation used to evoke another narrative," and the latter that "an allusion is made in order to evoke associations with the work, style or convention alluded to and thus to convey meaning."[37] With regard to Eshkeri's scores, allusion is used in the sense that Kassabian outlines, to describe quotations that bring narratives from other works to bear intertextually on the score. It is clear that there is some overlap between quotation and allusion, and whether borrowed material functions as one or the other will sometimes vary depending on the knowledge of the listener, but Eshkeri makes use of both within his writing.

Eshkeri's "Drive to the Boatyard" cue from *Layer Cake* makes use of material quoted in another of the film's cues, "Drive to the Warehouse," co-composed by Eshkeri and Lisa Gerrard. The quotation reinforces the links between the two scenes and also enmeshes Eshkeri's cue into the general sound of the film. The latter point is emphasized by a number of comments on a YouTube video of the latter cue that criticize the track for being incomplete—the elements these users seek are unique to the "Boat-house" cue, and are accordingly not present in the video that presents the "Warehouse" track. Whereas in that example Eshkeri quoted another part of the same film, he has also used very brief quotations to connect films together. His main title for *Johnny English Reborn* draws on the very open-ing of the equivalent theme to the original *Johnny English* film (composed by his one-time mentor, Ed Shearmur). However, it is the rhythmic and melodic profiles rather than the theme itself that are quoted—none of Shearmur's material appears in Eshkeri's theme—and Eshkeri develops his own title melody from this starting point (see Figure 2.7, below). The brevity of the quotation masks it somewhat, as does the fact that the as-cending minor scale that makes up the melody is a compositional feature that appears in a number of Eshkeri's scores, as has already been dis-cussed. There are two direct quotations of the original *Johnny English* theme in Eshkeri's score, during scenes which involve flashbacks to the earlier film. Both the "Opening" and "Mozambique" scenes feature the original Johnny English character, and the use of the original theme rein-forces this narrative connection.

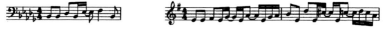

Figure 2.7. Start of Shearmur's *Johnny English* theme (left) and Eshkeri's *Johnny English Reborn* theme (right), showing the use of a brief quotation of the former in the latter

Quotation plays a significant function in the *Stardust* score, notably through the inclusion of a number of references to the nursery rhyme, *Twinkle, Twinkle Little Star*. Eshkeri credits Vaughn with its inclusion, as-serting that the director had the idea well before the film even went into production. Vaughn told him he had been playing *Twinkle* (as he called it) on the piano and was keen to see if they could integrate it into the film. As a result, "*Stardust* is covered in little secret *Twinkle, Twinkle Little Star* quotes, but they're quite difficult to spot by ear."[38] Some of the quotations are quite apparent, but others, as Eshkeri asserts, are hidden within the texture or harmony and are likely only to be identified through repeated close listening. The use of the theme will be considered in more detail in Chapter 5, but in general terms the quotation of such a well-known nursery rhyme melody reinforces the fantasy element of the score as well as linking closely to the subject matter of the film.[39]

Allusions within Eshkeri's score also vary from blatant to secret, though as with quotations, even those stated clearly are only apparent if the source is already known by the viewer. However, the viewer is not the only 'consumer' of the score, and Eshkeri admits that some of the time he inserts hidden quotations because "it is interesting for the players," a perspective that returns to his philosophy of collaboration and of valuing everyone who contributes to the creation of a film score.[40] He acknowledges that it is not always appropriate to include quotations and allusions, but that they can work well in "a fun score" such as *Stardust*.[41] Two examples from *Stardust* demonstrate the contrasting ways in which Eshkeri employs allusion in the score. Cue 1M8 "Victoria" accompanies a scene in which the character arrives at the village shop, pushes to the front of the queue and requests (or perhaps more accurately demands) her order from Tristan who is working behind the counter. The cue is just fourteen bars long consisting of a four-bar phrase, several bars of silence, and a complementary four-bar phrase, and all of the musical material is taken from Cherubino's aria, "Voi che sapete" from Mozart's *The Marriage of Figaro*. In the opera, Cherubino, the Count's page, is infatuated with the Countess and sings of the strange, unknown feelings he has in his heart:

> You who know what love is,
> women, see what I have in my heart,
> women, see what I have in my heart!
> I will explain what I am experiencing,
> It is new to me, I do not understand it.
> I feel an emotion full of desire,
> that is pleasure, and then is suffering.
> I feel frosty and then my soul is afire,
> and in a moment I am freezing again.
> I am looking for a something outside of me,
> I do not know who has it,
> I do not know what it is.
> I sigh and groan, without wanting to,
> I pulse and shake, without knowing it.[42]

Although neither the vocal line nor any of the lyric is present in Eshkeri's cue, which consists of the string accompaniment with an additional clarinet at the cadences, the allusion brings the meaning of the Mozart aria (and, to an extent, the whole opera) into the world of *Stardust* and applies it specifically to Tristan and his feelings for Victoria. By contrast, the allu-

sion employed in 7M70 "Fat Witch Dies" is hidden within the texture of
this original cue, as well as by sound effects in the film itself. Eshkeri plays
on the method of the witch's death—she is attacked and eaten by
wolves—embedding Prokofiev's "Wolf" motif from *Peter and the Wolf* into
the cue. The theme appears complete but in a modified form in the trumpets, before shorter variations are incorporated into the French horn and
low woodwind parts (see Figure 2.8, below). Some of the LMO players
who recorded the score will have detected Eshkeri's reference, though the
allusion is masked almost entirely by fast-moving string and wind parts
and it is extremely unlikely that it would be heard and understood by
many viewers of the film (the cue does not appear on the soundtrack album).

**Figure 2.8. Trumpet and horn parts from bars 54–59 of 7M70 "Fat
Witch Dies," showing the use of Prokofiev's "Wolf" theme**

Self-Referencing

The final type of pre-existing music that is referred to within Eshkeri's
scores is his own previous material. Self-borrowing (as termed by Bill
Wrobel)[43] has been part of musical composition for hundreds of years,
and even within film music it is not a new phenomenon. Though he
vehemently denied it, Bernard Herrmann recycled material between concert and film works,[44] and Benjamin Winters devotes a section of his book
on Erich Wolfgang Korngold's *The Adventures of Robin Hood* to the composer's sharing of material between and across his film and concert
scores.[45] Similarly, the opening motif of John Williams's score to *Star
Wars* (1977) returns with the addition of a single note in *E.T. the Extra
Terrestrial* (1982), as the music on which the "flying bicycles" theme is
based (see Figure 2.9, below), and a short cue from towards the end of
Trevor Jones's music for *Chains of Gold* (1991) is the inspiration for his
Gulliver's Travels (1996) main title. In the contemporary film industry the

re-use or referencing of older material may be a direct consequence of the immense pressure on a composer to produce the precise sound a director desires. This is especially the case if a film has been temped with the composer's own music, or if a studio or director has approached a composer precisely because they are looking for a score that sounds like one of the composer's past projects. A demo of older material submitted to win a film project may similarly place the composer in a position where the reuse of that material is a necessary part of creating the resulting score. Self-borrowing is also a natural consequence of the need to develop an individual voice and style, as well as providing a chance for music from small or under-appreciated projects to be brought to wider public attention and acclaim.

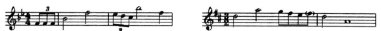

Figure 2.9. Opening motif of *Star Wars* and the first phrase of the "Flying Bicycles" theme from *E.T. the Extra Terrestrial*, both by John Williams

Stardust references some of Eshkeri's earliest material, notably his score for the BBC documentary film *Colosseum*. In addition to subtly shifting, drawn-out harmonic progressions, and the use of the French horn for music associated with grandeur and importance, two of the musical ideas present in *Stardust* can be related back to this earlier score. *Stardust*'s "Septimus" theme, which will be discussed in greater detail in Chapter 5, draws on similar material presented in *Colosseum* to accompany the opening of the arena itself. 2M12 "First Kill" is in ¼, but the *Stardust* cue derived from it is in ⅞, continuing a pattern established in the visuals of each brother being associated with the number inherent in their name (ranging from the number of buttons on their jackets to the members in their travelling parties). Eshkeri's consideration of this material may have resulted from Paramount's request for two *Stardust* demos at short notice, though there are strong narrative reasons for relating the theme to a cue from *Colosseum*. Not only is Septimus Latin for seventh, but the royal family to which the prince belongs can be seen to have its antecedents in the world of Ancient Rome inhabited by *Colosseum*, where accession was so often the result of murder, cunning and heartlessness. Accordingly, Eshkeri's reference to the material can be seen as an allusion, invoking the narrative of *Colosseum* to link Stormhold with Ancient Rome symbolically, and emphasizing his understanding of Septimus's character.

The other thematic connection between these two films presents the same potential for narrative links and allusion. 2M17 "Pugnate Part 2"

from *Colosseum* is the model for 7M72 "Zombie Fight" from *Stardust*, both
cues accompanying swordfights played out in front of rapt audiences (a
Roman crowd and ghostly princes respectively). Continued editing of the
visual footage during the period in which Eshkeri was composing the
score impacted significantly on the creation and development of 7M72,
leaving him very little time to construct the musical accompaniment to
this scene.[46] That said, the cue's pulsing quaver accompaniment relates it
to other material in the *Stardust* score, and there are points of close syn-
chronicity between accents in the music and parts of the duel, resulting in
the cue being properly embedded within the score and film.

The closing cue of Eshkeri's score for the German two-part television film *Ring of the Nibelungs* (2004, also known as *The Curse of the Ring* or
The Dark Kingdom: The Dragon King) can be seen as a melodic model for
one of the main thematic ideas in *Stardust*. "Todesfinale" is not only based
around a triadic figure, but also outlines a melodic shape that is a clear
forebear to 7M76/77 "Coronation Parts 1 & 2," as shown in Figure 2.10.
Just as with the material derived from *Colosseum*, the themes share narrative associations that lead to allusion: both accompany the transition between eras in their respective films.[47]

**Figure 2.10. "Todesfinale" from *Ring of the Nibelungs* (top), and
the start of 7M76/77 "Coronation Parts 1 & 2" from *Stardust* (bottom)**

Stardust is also the source for musical ideas found in some of Eshkeri's
later scores, one example being *The Snowman and the Snowdog* (2012). Moments of magic, such as the snowman and the snowdog coming to life,
are accompanied by music that recalls the presentation of magic in *Stardust*, with Eshkeri using the same harmonic progression and compositional techniques on both occasions.[48] In this instance the source is not a specific cue from the earlier film, but there is still a significant narrative
relationship between the two scores. As identified above, the reuse or
referencing of older material is a common compositional strategy in the
film-music industry. Eshkeri's skill in the selection of appropriate reference material from his back-catalogue demonstrates his understanding of
the business and an acute awareness of good practice among those in the
profession. Far from simply drawing on older themes at random, there is

clear evidence of careful consideration in the referencing of material that is a distinctive feature of his compositional approach.

Performance

This may appear to be an unusual characteristic to list within a film composer's stylistic traits, but it has a double meaning for Eshkeri. Firstly, he always records live performers rather than using an electronic sample orchestra in his film scores. A significant advantage of this philosophy is that all of his core team can contribute meaningfully to the final musical product, something that would not be possible if he produced a sample-based score. Despite being a made-for-television film with a fairly limited budget, his first professional score, *Colosseum*, was recorded by the LMO. As this emphasizes, Eshkeri's commitment to live music has been evident since the very start of his career, though he acknowledges there is sometimes an element of electronic sweetening that takes place, as is usual in the business.[49] Secondly, the element of performance is a key component in the way Eshkeri's scores are recorded. In interview, all of Eshkeri's core team spoke of the "performance" rather than "playing" of the music when referring to recording sessions. Conductor Andy Brown is keen to come "off click" as much as possible and allow the music space to breathe with the film, and it is through perceiving the sessions as performances that the "liveness" of the playing is captured in Steve McLaughlin's recording.

Musical Style and *Stardust*

Eshkeri's working relationship with director Matthew Vaughn on *Stardust* went far beyond what might normally be expected in terms of a composer/director collaboration. Music editor Daryl Kell recalls "that Matthew had a lot of trust [in Ilan], but at the same time was quite hands on," and discussions with the composer and with McLaughlin reinforce this perspective.[50] Vaughn often had a clear idea about exactly what the music should sound like, suggesting or choosing source music for inclusion, influencing the overall shape and thematic content of the score, providing detailed musical descriptions for some parts of the underscore, and even receiving a co-composition credit on one cue. Each of these types of interaction offers insight into the Eshkeri/Vaughn partnership, and the following discussion draws on examples from the *Stardust* score to analyze the impact of this collaborative relationship on Eshkeri's working methods and film-scoring approach and style.

As has already been noted, it was Vaughn who suggested that *Twinkle, Twinkle Little Star* might be integrated into the music for *Stardust*. Having approached Eshkeri with the initial suggestion, Vaughn went further, asking if it was possible to "do *Twinkle, Twinkle* in a sad way," to which Eshkeri responded by creating a minor version of the melody.[51] While there is perhaps nothing surprising in this outcome, Karlin and Wright note in *On the Track* that "if twelve composers write a romantic cue for twelve different films, you're going to get a lot of different takes on the meaning of romantic."[52] Eshkeri shares this view, but suggests that a close working relationship between composer and director can assist significantly when trying to deduce precisely what a director wants from a given set of instructions. He comments that

> if somebody says "I want a minor version of *Twinkle, Twinkle Little Star*" there's a million ways that you could approach that. But the right way to approach it is to understand what it is the director's aiming for within the boundaries of what the film is, what the budget is, what you can achieve, what's possible. What does he really mean, what is he really aiming for?[53]

Vaughn could almost certainly not have envisaged the melody appearing in quite so many different guises across the score. Eshkeri used his understanding of Vaughn's filmic vision to manipulate the theme so that it retains its basic shape, but is inflected variously towards minor, diminished, and occasionally minor/major tonalities. Repeated notes are omitted to leave the outline structure of the melody, and the third note is consistently flattened. The lowering of this pitch, the sixth degree of the scale, creates the "sad" effect that Vaughn desired, while also generating an air of exoticism and intrigue through the chromatic inflection of the melody. Sometimes only the opening figure is present, but Eshkeri often continues the melody, making further chromatic alterations to the descending scale that follows to reinforce or counter the opening minor tonality (see Figure 2.11). In this instance the impact of the director on the composer's approach can be clearly identified—Vaughn provided the concept, Eshkeri the understanding to translate that into the music Vaughn wanted. The influence of Vaughn's idea resulted in Eshkeri integrating another nursery rhyme snippet into the score without any specific instruction or suggestion from the director. At the start of cue 5M55 "Mouse Love," the opening two bars of *Three Blind Mice* are incorporated into the violin parts. The two phrases are presented quite clearly—there is nothing else in the texture at that point—but owing to them being simple three-note descending scales the reference is quite hard to identify without prior knowledge of its existence. Nonetheless, Eshkeri's gesture represents an 'in-joke' with the director, emphasizing the closeness of their relationship and a subtle integration of Vaughn's ideas into his own musical approach.

Figure 2.11. Melody of *Twinkle, Twinkle Little Star*, and one use in the *Stardust* score—bars 34–39 of 7M74 "Shining." Note how the initial minor tonality caused by the flat sixth (D♭) is countered by the major scale that follows it

Vaughn was instrumental in defining aspects of the film's musical structure, the director taking an active role in determining the use of some of Eshkeri's thematic material. The aforementioned "Septimus" theme and the French horn melody that opens the score will both be discussed in greater detail in later chapters, but are also worthy of inclusion here owing to Vaughn's influence over their use or lack thereof. Eshkeri conceived the 7/8 theme as relating to Septimus himself, but as the project progressed discussions between the composer and director led to a wider association of the musical material with all of the royal family of Stormhold, and by extension to the kingdom itself. Accordingly, the theme is sometimes heard within scenes that do not feature Septimus, something that would not have happened without Vaughn's input into the structure of the score. By contrast, Vaughn's integration into Eshkeri's collaborative music-making process resulted in the opening horn melody from the film's prologue never being heard again in the score. The composer had originally intended to return to the theme later in the film for Captain Shakespeare, but following discussions with the director it was even excised from the appearance of the film title at the end of the opening sequence, where Eshkeri had scored it in an early version of the cue. The effect of Vaughn's input into the structuring of the score is significant, not least because it resulted in the composer having to create a new theme for Captain Shakespeare, increasing his workload.

The closeness of this collaboration is perhaps most evident in cue 5M55 "Mouse Love," for which Vaughn not only gave Eshkeri a detailed description of what he wanted musically, but also became involved in the actual composition of part of the cue. Eshkeri recalls that Vaughn's instructions for the cue were that "it's like wedding music and it's like Pachelbel's *Canon*,"[54] to which the composer responded by creating a ground bass over which are woven string melodies that progress from crotchets to quavers in the style of the Pachelbel model.[55] The "wedding music" effect is created by the addition of ascending arpeggios in the harp part, the slow tempo that gives the music time to breathe and recalls the procession of a bridal party, and the delicate scoring for strings and harp. The cue exists in three different versions (5M55, 5M55 Alt and 5M55 Alt R), and this section, which also appears in an earlier cue, 2M10 "Picnic," is consistent across all interpretations.[56] Just as with the integration of *Twinkle, Twinkle Little Star*, Eshkeri quickly understood Vaughn's direction. The second half of 5M55 demonstrates a different aspect of this collaboration, however. The original cue is credited to Eshkeri, but that is not what is heard in the film.

> On *Stardust*, for example, there is one cue where I wrote it over and over again and Matthew was like, "no, but I've got this tune in my head." Eventually I sent him off with Bob [Robert Elhai] and I was like, "Bob is going to help you get this out of your head onto the paper." And so there's a cue called "The Mouse" [5M55 "Mouse Love"] that reaches a climax and then it's got a bit at the end of it. The bit at the end of it is written by Vaughn. To be honest, it's remarkably similar to what I'd been writing, but it was his idea and it was written by him, so on the actual score it says Ilan Eshkeri and Matthew Vaughn, which he was always slightly embarrassed about.[57]

Eshkeri may have overstated Vaughn's embarrassment at the co-composition credit—the director remarks "I wrote this piece of music with Ilan"[58] on his Blu-ray commentary with co-writer Jane Goldman—but his view that Vaughn's music is "remarkably similar" to his original cue is certainly accurate. The alternate version simplifies some of the movement in the accompaniment and removes a little melodic material in the woodwind, effectively rendering it a variation of 5M55 rather than a new composition. Nonetheless, it represents another facet of the collaboration between director and composer and emphasises the effect that a director can have on a composer's work.

Film Score and Film Song

Vaughn also influenced the music of *Stardust* by approaching Take That to write and perform the film's closing credit song.[59] In the introduction to *Popular Music and Film*, Ian Inglis comments that "the use of popular music as a soundtrack device, or as the provider of a theme song, is now commonplace,"[60] and in the contemporary industry films with orchestral scores will often close with a pop song. However, Ronald H. Sadoff, reports that "it is not a common practice to commission a song from a major pop artist, for a film,"[61] a point that is emphasised by a paucity of scholarly writing on the subject.[62] Accordingly, Vaughn's decision to approach Take That about writing a new song specifically for *Stardust* marks a departure from normal practice that brought potential drawbacks as well as benefits.

The interpolation of popular music into a film usually results in a synergistic relationship, Lee Barron defining this as the "practice by which media products can be utilised to advertise or support other media products."[63] In addition to this cross-promotion, financial risk can be somewhat defrayed owing to the generation of multiple products and revenue streams.[64] A featured track would normally be drawn from an artist's existing repertoire, offering easy identification for film viewers and a degree of knowledge for the production companies regarding the potential success of a new release. The film composer would usually have access to the songs before and during the composition of the score, enabling the tailoring of the music to flow smoothly with the interpolations, and their easy integration into the musical fabric of the film. By commissioning a new song, Vaughn risked losing some of the financial benefits of using older material, though the risk was lessened somewhat by his choice of an extremely popular band. However, Eshkeri was perhaps slightly disadvantaged since the song was not available to him when composing the majority of the film's orchestral score. Vaughn confirms that the song was written late in post-production when he discusses it on the Blu-ray director commentary, saying Take That "saw the film and loved it and wrote a song in five days and played it to us, and we thought it was great."[65] Richard Lancaster, recording engineer on *Stardust*, reveals that Take That recorded *Rule the World* in Abbey Road Studio 2 on 22 May 2007.[66] This was the penultimate day of recording for the whole film project, emphasising how late in the post-production process the song was written.

Eshkeri's relationship with Take That is somewhat difficult to quantify since the band was approached so close to the end of the project. However, there is evidence of shared concepts and shared musical material, and of both soundtrack contributors working towards similar goals in the creation of the music. As will be shown in Chapter 5, Eshkeri's score is based principally around the musical material created to represent Tristan, and *Rule the World* adopts a similar perspective. The lyrics are presented from the man's perspective, emphasised by the male voices of the band members and lines such as "if you stay with me, girl," which refer to the female partner in relation to the man. Like the score, the song also endeavours to highlight specific aspects of the narrative. It includes the breaking down of walls (something that happens metaphorically in the film, though the final scene indicates it may also have occurred literally), repeated references to stars, and, of course, Tristan's destiny as outlined in the song's title. One further possible connection to the story can be found in Gary Barlow's performance. During the second verse he elides the words "if angels," the aural result of which is that the first two syllables can be heard as the name "Yvaine," though it is unclear whether or not this character reference is deliberate. Such a close narrative relationship between a film and its song is extremely unusual, and is a key benefit of the song being composed specifically for the picture.

There is also some direct musical connectivity between song and score. Eshkeri met with Take That to listen to the song and discuss linking it with the orchestral score, the result of which is the final cue of the underscore, 7M78 "Coronation Part 3." The cue is Eshkeri's arrangement of the chords from the chorus of *Rule the World*, and credits Gary Barlow as composer, Eshkeri as arranger, and Elhai as orchestrator. The cue functions as a transition from one musical realm to another, neatly drawing on elements of both sound worlds to create coherence, while also bringing the orchestral music to a conclusion and introducing the closing credit song. The harmonic progression is syncopated in Take That's song, but Eshkeri rationalises it to bring it in line with the way in which other progressions such as the "star" chords operate—one chord per bar, with occasional changes on the half bar (see Figure 2.12, below). Additionally, he thickens the harmony in places through the addition of 9ths, inflecting the chords in a similar manner to the aforementioned "star" chords, which include a combination of added 6ths, 7ths and 9ths. There is no melodic line of note in the cue, which underscores the final voiceover of the film, but movement is present in the form of ascending arpeggios. These string lines mirror the vast descending lines that accompany the falling star towards the start of the film (2M14A Part 2), as Tristan and Yvaine become stars themselves and ascend into the night sky, and also match the ascending arpeggios heard as the couple dance aboard the Caspartine in a scene that also features a camera pan up to the heavens (5M45B). 7M78 also recalls the harp arpeggios and cyclic chord progression of the Pachelbel's *Canon*-inspired "Mouse Love" cue, in a final reinforcement of the unending love of the film's protagonists. However, even within this cue there is evidence of the difficulties posed by the song not being available until very late in the process.

Rule the World is in B minor (with the chorus in D major), but since 7M78 follows 7M76/77 without a break, it is therefore obliged to continue where the previous cue finished harmonically, placing it in C major. The closing cues were recorded on the final few days in the studio, and Eshkeri considered ways in which he could transpose part of the sequence or include a modulation earlier in the run of cues to ensure the score ended in a closer related key to the song. However, in the event it was felt that the silence between the end of the score and the start of the song was sufficient to remove any harmonic tension caused by the abrupt change from C major to B minor.

Figure 2.12. Comparison of the harmonic structures of the chorus to *Rule the World* (top) and 7M78 "Coronation Part 3" from *Stardust* (bottom)

Conclusions

As this chapter has shown, Eshkeri's diversity of film-scoring projects has not precluded the cultivation of a unique musical style and identity. This is not to suggest that his style is static—the continued variety of films on which he works inevitably results in a development of his working methods, sound, techniques and approaches—but the findings of this chapter serve to outline the parameters within which a past project such as *Stardust* may be interpreted. The score was impacted by decisions taken during the film's production process including the process of adaptation from novel to screenplay, some of which are expounded in further detail in Chapter 3. Similarly, as a fantasy feature film produced in the post-*Lord of the Rings* era, establishing the critical context in which *Stardust* exists provides a foundation for the analysis and reading of Eshkeri's score in Chapter 5.

3

CRITICAL CONTEXT OF THE BOOK, FILM, AND NARRATIVE

Author Neil Gaiman and artist Charles Vess first collaborated in 1989, when Vess provided illustrations for some issues of Gaiman's *Books of Magic* and *Sandman* series, both published by DC Comics. In addition to laying the foundations of their partnership, their work on *Sandman* played a crucial, though fortuitous role in the conception of the *Stardust* story. *Sandman* issue 19, "A Midsummer Night's Dream," was awarded the World Fantasy Award for "Best Short Story" in 1991,[1] and it was while the pair were at an after-awards party in Tucson, Arizona, that Gaiman was inspired. He recalled the origins of the *Stardust* story in an article in *USA Today* in July 2007, a week before the film's US release:

> The British-born Gaiman was at a party, stargazing, when he saw it: "In England I'd seen shooting stars, and they were like a streak of light across the sky. Now I'm out in the desert, and what I'm seeing is a meteor coming fairly close with no light pollution anywhere, and it's like a diamond coming down. I'm watching it fall, somewhere over there—10 to 20 miles away. And I'm thinking, 'my God, I just saw a falling star, and I know where it fell. I could go and find it.' Then there was this weird 'what-if' moment, and I thought: 'what if when I found it, it wasn't a little lump of meteoric iron? What if it was a girl? What if she was the falling star? What if she had a broken leg? And what if she was (angry)?'" Gaiman says with a laugh. "Suddenly I had a story."[2]

Gaiman returned to the party, sought out Vess and explained the concept to him, and the two agreed to collaborate on the project. He reiterates this scenario in "The Quest for the Stone...," a special feature on the Blu-ray release of *Stardust*, where he links it to a memory of driving in Ireland with his wife, seeing a stone wall with a gap in it, and thinking "wouldn't it be cool if [. . .] just a hole in the wall away was fairyland?"[3]

Stardust originated as a four-book prestige-comic mini-series published by DC Comics in 1997–98. The story was re-released as a hardback illustrated book titled Stardust: Being a Romance Within the Realms of Faerie by the same company in October 1998, and won the 1999 "Mythopoeic Fantasy Award for Adult Literature."[4] A non-illustrated version of Stardust was produced by Spike Avon Books the following year, and received the American Literary Association's "Alex Award" in 2000 as one of "ten books written for adults that have special appeal to young adults, ages twelve through eighteen."[5] The book has been reprinted several times since the turn of the millennium, but the most significant change since the transfer from graphic to non-illustrated novel occurred with the production of Matthew Vaughn's filmic adaptation in 2007. Gaiman was involved in the film project as part of the screenwriting team, but there are numerous alterations to and embellishments of the plot and characters between the book and film. The following critical evaluation of Stardust proceeds from the novel through the process of adaptation to the film, enabling the identification and discussion of key narrative developments, additions and omissions. The film is then contextualised as a twenty-first century fantasy feature, ahead of a similar consideration of the musical score in Chapter 5.

Neil Gaiman's *Stardust*

Gaiman's novel begins with a prologue set seventeen years earlier than the body of the story, during the early years of the reign of Queen Victoria.[6] The story opens in the village of Wall, so named because of the stone wall to the east of the village that separates it from the magical land of Faerie. Access to Faerie is only possible through the single gap in the stone, located just north of the village itself, but this is guarded at all times and access to Faerie is generally forbidden. The exception is on May Day every nine years, when a travelling market visits the meadow across the wall. The villagers mix with the inhabitants of Faerie on these rare occasions, and it is at one such market that Dunstan Thorn meets a stallholder's servant girl, their liaison resulting in the birth of a son, Tristran. The main body of the story begins seventeen years later, and concerns Tristran's adventures in Faerie. He wishes to win the hand of Victoria Forester whom he believes to be "the most beautiful girl in the British Isles [. . .] if not the world,"[7] and he attempts to woo her as he walks her home from the village shop one October evening. Tristran speaks at length of the distances he would travel for Victoria, but she rebuffs his advances until he promises to bring her a star they see fall to the east, across the wall.[8]

Meanwhile, in Faerie, the eighty-first Lord of Stormhold despairs that he cannot simply pass on his title to a sole remaining heir since three of his sons are still alive (having murdered the other four). To solve this problem he enchants his topaz necklace and throws it into the night sky, declaring that whoever retrieves the Power of Stormhold shall be the next Lord. The necklace collides with a star, causing it to fall (as observed by Tristran and Victoria) and starting the brothers Primus, Tertius and Septimus on their quests. The falling star is divined by three ancient witch queens, the Lilim, who live in an old hut in the woods of Faerie. Keen to regain their long-lost youth by consuming the star's heart, the oldest eats the remains of the last star they captured some two hundred years before, temporarily restoring her youth and magical powers. She similarly sets off for the star, setting the third and final branch of the story into motion.

Tristran meets unusual people in Faerie, such as a "little hairy person"[9] who is part of a secret organisation called the Fellowship of the Castle. He also discovers that he knows the direction of any place in Faerie when asked where that place is, even if he previously had no knowledge that such a location even existed. Nursery rhymes from Tristran's childhood also play a key role during his travels in Faerie, and his knowledge of *How Many Miles to Babylon* enables him to quickly cross the great distance between the wall and the fallen star. However, instead of a lump of cosmic rock, Tristran encounters a young woman called Yvaine, who does not take kindly to his plans to present her as a prize to Victoria. Early in their journey to Wall they encounter a scene from another nursery rhyme, *The Lion and the Unicorn*, in which the creatures battle for the crown. At Yvaine's request Tristran intervenes, saving the life of the unicorn, guided in his actions by his knowledge of the children's tale.

The three strands of the story converge at the witch queen's inn, a structure created by magic and designed as a trap for the star. Yvaine arrives on the unicorn, followed by Primus and Tristran in the prince's coach.[10] Tristran is saved from poison by the unicorn, and although Primus refuses the witch queen's food and drink for fear of poisoning (it being Septimus's preferred form of murder), he dies at her hand when he inadvertently comes between her and the star. The witch queen traps Tristran and Yvaine in the inn, revealing her true intentions, but they escape using the last of the Babylon candle, leaving the inn just as the witch prepares to kill Yvaine. The final part of the story is considered in detail below, in the discussion concerning changes made to the narrative during the process of adaptation.

Adaptation: From Book to Film

Derek Paget suggests that "discussion of film/TV adaptations of novels is often troubled by the vexed question of fidelity to 'prior texts' deemed to have inherently greater cultural standing."[11] The question of "fidelity" to the source material is one that persists despite,. as Brian McFarlane notes, "the concept not merely being dismissed but discredited at length" in the majority of texts on literary adaptation.[12] However, McFarlane continues, observing that the reason this concept is still debated may be that "no amount of serious discourse ever really disposes of the discontent expressed in 'it wasn't like that in the book.'"[13] The comment is made slightly tongue-in-cheek, but he raises a significant issue for someone attempting to adapt a well-known work of literature:

> It may be that, even among the most rigorously high-minded of film viewers confronted with the film version of a cherished novel or play, it is hard to suppress a sort of yearning for a faithful rendering of *one's own vision of the literary text*.[14]

Even in the case of a graphic novel such as *Stardust*, not all aspects of the plot are presented in fine detail, and there is still some space left in the narration for the imagination of the reader. So to whose interpretation should a film be "faithful"? The film director's? The original author's? Even in the latter case, there would inevitably still be those who felt that the film did not meet their expectations having read the book. Additionally, since a book allows for a broad range of interpretations, there seems to be no good reason why the view of the author should suddenly be promoted as "correct" in an adaptation.[15] As Deborah Cartmell states, "we read adaptations for their generation of a plurality of meanings. Thus the intertextuality of the adaptation is our primary concern."[16]

Intertextuality exists not just between the novel and the film, but also within each of the various canons and genres with which either version of story may be associated. The original *Stardust*, a graphic novel, can be contextualized generally by a knowledge of that genre, and more specifically by other works by Neil Gaiman, particularly those with illustrations by Charles Vess. Similarly, it sits within Gaiman's general literary output and can be related to his other works as well as influences on his writing such as C.S. Lewis's *The Chronicles of Narnia*.[17] Readings of the film of *Stardust* may inevitably be influenced by the large number of fantasy and comic-book films and adaptations that have been released since *The Fellowship of the Ring* in 2001 (which include big-screen versions of three of the *Narnia* stories). The film also sits within the output of director Matthew Vaughn, as well as other films and television programs with which prominent members of cast or crew have been associated, something Vaughn takes advantage of in the casting of both Robert De Niro and Ricky Gervais.

The following section considers the ways in which *Stardust* was adapted for film by screenwriters Vaughn, Gaiman and Jane Goldman. Narrative divergences between the novel and film are discussed and rationalized where possible, to ascertain the fundamental ways in which the film is a genuine adaptation, rather than a copy of the literary original.

Matthew Vaughn's *Stardust*

Pre-Production

> Gaiman has resisted many studio efforts to adapt his work: he doesn't want the tales dragged into the realm of the big screen, only to be ruined. "You have to find someone you trust and let them go on with it. The alternative is 'give me a check, and do whatever you want.' But the pain, if that goes wrong, is too great," he says.[18]

Matthew Vaughn and Neil Gaiman first met in 2002 a year before Vaughn produced *A Short Film about John Bolton*, written and directed by Gaiman.[19] Vaughn was introduced to *Stardust* a couple of years later by his wife, Claudia Schiffer, who had read Gaiman's book, and Vaughn immediately approached the author about making a film.[20] He was not the first to appreciate the story's filmic potential—Miramax held the film rights during the late 1990s but Gaiman retrieved them when the option expired, and he resisted numerous other approaches prior to Vaughn's request.[21] Vaughn's "obvious love for the material and [his] creative ideas" were key to Gaiman even considering his request, and the writer felt he could trust the filmmaker to do it justice.[22]

Gaiman recalls that Vaughn's initial intention was to produce the film, and that the two of them approached Terry Gilliam about directing the picture. However, Gilliam "had just come off *Brothers Grimm* and he wasn't going to make another fairy tale for love or money. So Matthew became the director almost by accident."[23] Gaiman put Vaughn in touch with British novelist Jane Goldman, and the two of them set to work on the script.[24] *Variety* announced on 25 October 2005 that Vaughn and Paramount were "in final negotiations" with regard to him directing and producing the film of *Stardust*, for which the script was already complete, and drew comparisons with other fantasy films such as *The Princess Bride* and *The Neverending Story*.[25] Gaiman has stated that *The Princess Bride* inspired him to try and create a fairy tale for adults,[26] and it also figures in

Vaughn's overarching vision for the film. In an interview with Edward Douglas for the website SuperHeroHype.com, given in the days preceding the US premiere of the film, Vaughn revealed his take on the structure of the narrative:

> I just read it and I felt like I could make my version of *The Princess Bride*. Basically, when I read it, it reminded me of *Princess Bride* and it reminded me of a movie called *Midnight Run* and I just felt I could combine the two and do something different and unique. [. . .] The *Midnight Run* bit came from, if you think about this very quickly, the star is the Charles Grodin character and Tristan is the De Niro character sent by the bail bondsmen (which is Victoria) to go bring them back. They're hand-cuffed together, and this time, it's the silver chain, and then you [have] got the FBI, which is the princes trying to catch them, and then you've got the mob who's trying to kill them, which is the witch. [. . .] Most people think I'm insane when I tell them that, but I'd just thought, "I want to do *Princess Bride* with a *Midnight Run* overtone."[27]

Vaughn's interpretation is somewhat eccentric, but his ability to visualize the plot similarities between *Stardust* and *Midnight Run* shows a thorough understanding of the interweaving narratives in films. He also described the film as "*Pirates of the Caribbean* meets *The Princess Bride*," noting that he hoped *Stardust* would "[match] *Pirates* in terms of the swashbuckling action and [special] effects." The first draft of the script was written in just two weeks, finance was secured around two months later,[28] and the scriptwriting team was enlarged to three when Gaiman himself joined the project to assist with refining the screenplay.[29] He was also involved in decisions regarding casting and the selection of locations for filming.[30] On 6 March 2006 *Variety* announced that Charlie Cox, Clare Danes, Sienna Miller, Robert De Niro and Michelle Pfeiffer had joined the *Stardust* cast, and production would start the following month in the UK and Iceland.[31]

Production

> "I don't believe there is any moral high ground in reproducing some-thing exactly," Gaiman says. "I would hate for people to go and see a [film] version of *Stardust* that is *Stardust* the book, only not as good."[32]

> We all know cinema is a very different medium to books, and I think you have to make a good film first and foremost for people who haven't read the book or don't know the book, more than making a good movie for people who love the book and want it to be treated as a "hallow ground"—don't muck with the story or the structure. I always respected the soul of the book.[33]

While Vaughn may have "respected the soul of the book," he was not afraid to make changes to the story or characters in order to "make a good film first and foremost." However, as Gaiman remarks in the above quotation, and as the previous discussion of literary adaptation has shown, changes are a necessary requirement of converting a narrative from novel to film. Novels and films move at different paces, and whereas the former offers a mix of dialogue, narration and description, the latter is reliant principally on dialogue for the telling of the story. The book contains an extended prelude that is radically condensed in the film to enable Tristran (now renamed Tristan, introducing both mythological and Wagnerian intertextuality) to enter the action more quickly.[34] A voiceover is utilised in the opening scenes to clarify aspects of the narrative premise regarding the wall (which may not be crossed under any circumstances), this filmic method of storytelling offering a quick way of covering the necessary narrative ground. Similarly, the three main intersecting storylines are introduced in a single sequence that cross-cuts between Tristan and Victoria, the princes, and Lamia, emphasising that the falling star is perceived simultaneously by all of the key characters. Again, the use of specifically filmic techniques enables the efficient establishment of the story's main narrative premise, something that takes nearly twenty pages of text in the book.[35]

The world beyond the wall, despite already being a fantastical realm, undergoes changes in Vaughn's adaptation. The whole of the magical world is renamed Stormhold, and the eighty-first Lord is upgraded to King. Accordingly, rather than becoming ruler of a region of Faerie, whoever retrieves the necklace (now ruby, rather than topaz) will become monarch of the entire country/world on that side of the wall, heightening the importance of the jewel to those in the chase. The scene with the dying King opens with him surrounded by three living sons, as in the book, but in the film the not-yet-dead Secundus then arrives to a triumphant fanfare. Vaughn has said that he wanted a recognisable actor for Secundus—he is played by Rupert Everett—precisely so that viewers would allot him some importance on his appearance,[36] and Eshkeri's score adds further weight to these expectations.[37] The King asks him what he can see from the window, intimating (to yet more triumphant music) that it will be Secundus who succeeds him as ruler, so when he is pushed to his death by Septimus to the King's amusement, it comes as quite a surprise. By casting Everett, Vaughn invites each member of the audience to draw on their own knowledge of the actor and apply layers of meaning and signification onto the character of Secundus. When he dies within a minute of his arrival (though he continues in the film as a ghost alongside his dead brothers) it causes viewers to question the role and status of every other character, and brings new interpretations and perspectives to bear on the narrative.

Another significant character adaptation is the augmentation and development of Captain Johannes Alberic, recast by Vaughn and Goldman as the fearsome Captain Shakespeare (Robert De Niro). Whereas Tristran and Yvaine's time aboard the Free Ship Perdita is covered in little over four pages in Gaiman's novel, the episode with Shakespeare and his pirate crew aboard the Caspartine is significantly extended in the film. It even continues beyond the departure of the protagonists with the "Can Can" sequence. The motivation of the characters is also quite different in the two versions of the flying ship scene, owing to small changes in background aspects of the narrative. In the novel, Captain Alberic informs Tristran that

> it wasn't entirely fortune that we found you. [. . .] It'd also be true to say that I was keeping half an eye out for you. I and a few others about the place. [. . .] Think of it as a fellowship.[38]

Tristran is able to connect the Captain to another character he met on his first day in Faerie, a "little hairy man with a hat and an enormous pack of goods," and the implication is that there is a secret organisation working behind the scenes in Faerie to help Tristran achieve his mission.[39] Whether the concept of a "fellowship" strayed too close to *The Lord of the Rings* for Vaughn and Goldman's liking, or whether it was simply a matter of removing some of the more passive characters in order to tighten the narrative arc of the film, the "little hairy man" is absent from the film, and with him disappears all trace of a support organisation for Tristan within Stormhold. Indeed, rather than being rescued from the cloud on which they accidentally find themselves, Tristan and Yvaine are captured by Shakespeare, and are only released from the ship's brig when Tristan reveals under questioning that they are heading for Wall, and beyond it, England. The difference is important since the characters in the book seem honor-bound to assist the travellers, whereas those in the film ultimately help and defend them because they earn the respect of the crew during their time aboard ship.

Despite being the principal antagonist, the witch queen receives relatively little attention in the novel. Gaiman's writing is elusive in its description of the three women—the Lilim—considering them both singly and as a trio as the witch-queen (always in the singular) and stating that their names were lost many years ago under the sea. He alludes to their reflections in the large mirror that stands in their hut, but questions whether they are, in fact, reflections, whether they are different people, or whether the women in the hut are actually the reflections of those in the mirror. Much of this ambiguity is removed in the film, and while this perhaps results in a loss of mysticism it greatly assists the writers in developing the involvement of all three of the Lilim (in the film their reflections are precisely that). Vaughn and Goldman name the witches for the Greek demigoddesses Lamia, Mormo and Empusa, embodying them with strong mythological signification. These names also create an impression of timelessness and power, mitigating to an extent the loss of mystique that results from their adaptation for screen.[40]

There are occasional scenes in the film where the integration of aspects of the book has caused narrative difficulties. In the novel, Tristran's ability to locate places is introduced within the context of his early adventure in Faerie with the little hairy man, and fits smoothly into the gradual development of his character. It also links him loosely to the Lords of Stormhold—Septimus is noted to have "some of the locating ability that ran, patchily, in his family line"—a trait not referred to in the film.[41] As already observed, the little hairy man is excised from the film of *Stardust*, and the adventure in which Tristan's ability is discovered is accordingly also absent from the screen adaptation. While this does not affect the overall story negatively (it actually serves to tighten it considerably), it leaves no reason for his innate sense of direction. A conversation between Tristan and Yvaine during a scene in the woods when on their way to Wall highlights this problem:

> **Yvaine:** Right. So let me get this straight. You think you know we're going the right way because, and I quote, "I just do."
>
> **Tristan:** I do though. I don't know why. Maybe it's my love for Victoria guiding me home. [. . .] We're going north, the wall is north. And if you look up in the sky even during the day you can see the . . . the evening star. . . . [He looks at the sky but cannot locate the star] That's so weird!
>
> **Yvaine:** That's funny. Hilarious. My sides are splitting.[42]

While Tristan's suggestion that he is guided by true love may be touching, it must be dismissed as entirely inaccurate since it is Yvaine, not Victoria who ultimately makes that claim on him. His practical reason for knowing where he is going is equally flawed by his inability to perceive Yvaine for all that she is, as he searches the sky for the star that trails behind him through the woods. Their journeying stops immediately after this conversation, Tristan heading into a nearby village for supplies and leaving Yvaine chained to a tree so she cannot run away, and they do not control the next stages of their journeys. Yvaine is rescued by a unicorn that carries her (inadvertently) to Lamia's inn, while Tristan manages to obtain passage with Primus, also arriving at the inn though via the road rather than through the forest. With this in mind it might reasonably be argued that Tristan does not, in fact, know where he is going during this scene, which calls into question why the scriptwriters tried to retain this aspect of his character in the first place. The only other time that he finds his way to a location without any explanation of how he achieves this is when he races to Lamia's lair towards the end of the film to rescue Yvaine from the witches. The shooting of the film indicates that he cannot have simply followed Lamia's coach, since it leaves the area around the gap in the wall long before Tristan reaches it. The guard recalls what he saw transpire, delaying him further, and yet Tristan and then Septimus arrives in plenty of time to interrupt the witches' sacrifice. This narrative wrinkle remains unexplained, but it is lost within the vast transformation of the story's climax and finale that occurs between book and film.[43]

The Third Act

> I wrote a very, what I call a rough, rough draft and it took about two weeks, and totally changed the third act. The third act in the book just was not cinematic. It just ended in a very sort of unheroic and not terribly exciting but sweet way, which just wasn't good enough for a film.[44]

As the above statement from Vaughn indicates, it is in the closing scenes that the story undergoes the most significant adaptation in the transfer from page to screen. The narratives begin to separate after the scene at the inn in which the witch queen (Lamia in the film) murders Primus, and Tristan and Yvaine escape the trap only to end up stranded on a cloud.

Septimus arrives at the site of the inn the following morning in both versions, finding his brother's dead body but not the stone he seeks. In the novel he is forced to postpone his quest for the stone in order to avenge Primus's murder (since it was not committed by a member of the family), and to this end he sets out to track the witch queen, eventually locating her at Diggory's Dyke. His plans for vengeance fail, however, and the witch kills him resulting in the apparent end of the quest for the Power of Stormhold. Tristran and Yvaine enjoy their brief episode with Captain Alberic, and once back on land encounter Madame Semele/Ditchwater Sal. Sal offers safe passage to the wall in exchange for Tristran's glass snowdrop, which is a powerful protecting charm rather than a mere trinket, turning him into a dormouse for the duration of the trip to save on space and food. She ignores Yvaine completely throughout this episode, owing to a curse placed on Sal by the witch queen that she should not perceive the star even if it should be right in front of her. Sal's caravan passes through Diggory's Dyke shortly after the witch queen has killed Septimus, and the queen forces Sal to reveal her travelling party:

> Madame Semele felt the words being torn from her mouth, whether she could say them or no. "There are the two mules who pull my caravan, myself, a maid-servant I keep in the form of a large bird, and a young man in the form of a dormouse."
>
> "Anyone else? Anything else?"
>
> "No one and nothing. I swear it upon the Sisterhood."
>
> The woman at the side of the road pursed her lips. "Then get away with you, and get along with you," she said.[45]

There is another occupant of the caravan—Yvaine—but the witch queen's curse means that Sal does not know this and therefore does not declare her presence. With this exchange the queen's last meaningful opportunity to capture the star is lost, all as a result of her own curse.[46] Their final meeting occurs at the market near the wall, by which time the witch's powers are completely drained and Yvaine has already given her heart to Tristran, placing it beyond the queen's reach. After much procrastination Tristran and Yvaine eventually journey to Stormhold where Tristran takes up his position as the eighty-second Lord, Yvaine succeeding him on his death. The narrative strands are concluded in turn—lords/princes, witches, protagonists—resulting in the "not terribly exciting, but sweet" ending identified by Vaughn.

By contrast, in the film the aftermath of the inn scene sets all of the principal characters on a collision course that ultimately leads to a dramatic climax at the witches' lair (which is an opulent palace rather than a ramshackle hut in the woods). In addition to finding Primus's body at the inn site, Septimus discovers that the carrier of the Stormhold necklace is a fallen star. Rather than avenge his brother's death, his thoughts turn to potential immortality for himself as ruler of Stormhold, adding greater strength to his desire to locate Yvaine. In contrast to her diminished role in the novel, Lamia also continues to play an active role in the story after the scene at the inn, though she does not feature particularly in the immediate aftermath of her failed trap. Tristan and Yvaine's time with Captain Shakespeare is fundamental to the development of their individual characters and relationship. It is while aboard the sky vessel that Tristan learns to handle a sword and we see him start to change from a boy to a man under the Captain's tutelage. Similarly Yvaine is humanised by the experience—she is seen eating (something Gaiman's star does not do), learning both piano and dancing, and joining in with the harvesting of lightning and other activities with the crew. Tristan and Yvaine warm to each other in the comfortable environment aboard ship, each becoming aware of some of their own shortcomings. In the absence of witches and any talk of Victoria Forester they are also able to learn more about each other. Yvaine's changing disposition towards Tristan is shown by the light radiating from her as they dance on the deck—a device used throughout the film to indicate her happiness—and as Shakespeare brings the sky vessel down onto the water Tristan and Yvaine are seen in a *Titanic*-esque position at the prow of the boat (though they are rather unromantically soaked as the Caspartine touches down).

Just as in the book Tristan and Yvaine meet Ditchwater Sal, but their journey to the market near the wall is uneventful. However, a miscommunication between Tristan and Yvaine the following morning leads her to believe that he has gone into the village of Wall to see his true love, Victoria, when he has actually gone to tell her he is no longer interested in her because he has found his true love, Yvaine. In desperation, Yvaine heads towards the wall herself and is only stopped from crossing (and becoming a pile of cosmic rock and dust) by Sal's servant, the Lady Una, who hijacks the caravan while Sal sleeps and rides to intercept the star. Lamia arrives at the wall before Tristan returns, and after she kills Sal in a short magical battle (which frees Lady Una from Sal's service), she kidnaps Yvaine and Una and heads for her lair.[47] Tristan is told what happened by the wall guard and gives chase on Sal's horse, but not before spotting and retrieving the glass snowdrop charm from the caravan. Septimus also reaches the gap in the wall, surveying the scene briefly before he too races after his prize.

The final dénouement occurs in the witches' lair. Lady Una is revealed to be Septimus's sister and Tristan's mother, and Septimus and Tristan kill Empusa and Mormo respectively before the prince is defeated by Lamia who drowns him using a voodoo doll. Tristan fights and is beaten by Lamia, but instead of killing him she chooses to release her captives, citing the deaths of her sisters as rendering her mission pointless. Her trick is designed to reinvigorate the star's heart, which she still plans to consume, but her plan backfires. Yvaine's reunion with Tristan mends her broken heart (she thought he had left her for Victoria) enabling her to shine, the light filling the cavernous space and turning Lamia to dust as she approaches the couple with her knife.[48] In the aftermath, Tristan retrieves the ruby necklace and is revealed as the next King of Stormhold, releasing the ghosts from their limbo.[49] He and Yvaine are crowned in a closing coronation scene that not only shows Tristan's parents reunited but also has those from both sides of the wall in attendance (including a rather disgruntled Victoria Forester). A voiceover delivers a short epilogue that details the end of Tristan and Yvaine's reign, once their descendants are adults themselves, at which point they use a Babylon candle and both become stars. Whereas Gaiman's witch-queen warns Yvaine that "your boy will break [your heart], or waste it, or lose it," the filmic voiceover instead suggests that "they ruled for eighty years, but no man can live forever. Except he who possesses the heart of a star, and Yvaine had given hers to Tristan completely."[50]

Post-Production

Vaughn was able to bring onto *Stardust* a large number of professionals with whom he had worked on previous projects. Jason Flemyng, who plays Primus in *Stardust* and who has appeared in several Vaughn films, notes that the director likes to take his technicians with him from project to project, Vaughn himself asserting that "if you've got a good crew, keep using them."[51] Vaughn recalls Paramount advising him initially to bring personnel with experience of creating large-budget films into key roles to replace his team from *Layer Cake*. Partly because of his negative experience on *X-Men 3*, Vaughn rejected this guidance and remained committed to his crew, particularly since they already understood and operated well within his preferred working methods. Vaughn was also keen to have Eshkeri compose the score for *Stardust*, so much so that he had first spoken with the composer before finance was even secured for the project. However, executives at Paramount were unconvinced of Eshkeri's suitability and refused to sanction the appointment, creating an impasse despite a lack of other composers under consideration for the commission. Eshkeri's lack of previous experience in the genre and his relatively low profile in the industry at the time will doubtless have contributed to the studio's position, particularly considering the importance attached to music to help bring out the fantasy in movies of this type. Steve McLaughlin recalls that Vaughn fought hard for Eshkeri to be given a chance to score the film:

> Vaughn, to his credit, was just not accepting anyone else. Because he was saying, "well look, can I have John Williams for it," and they [Paramount] said "no, he won't do it." He said, "well, there's John Williams and then if I can't get the top guy in the world then why can't I use my own guy? Because everyone else is going to be your choice."[52]

The situation was not resolved before Vaughn began shooting the film in April 2006, but he invited Eshkeri to spend time on the set in any case. The composer drafted some initial ideas while embedded within the project, but it was not until July that Paramount finally consented to approach him for some demo material. McLaughlin believes the studio hoped the demos would prove to Vaughn that Eshkeri was incapable of scoring the film, but the two cues he presented, "Septimus" and "The Flying Vessel," both appear in the final film albeit in slightly altered forms. Despite this, resistance remained and when shooting was completed in September 2006 the situation remained unresolved.[53]

The timeline for the period between summer 2006 and the end of the year is somewhat unclear, but the studio remained steadfastly against Eshkeri's appointment. Executive Vice-President of Music, Randy Spendlove, became involved with the project in late November 2006, and suggested that John Ottman, who had scored Twentieth Century Fox's *Fantastic Four* and Warner Brothers' *Superman Returns* in the previous two years, was an ideal choice to create the music for Paramount's offering into the fantasy canon. Owing to Spendlove's seniority within Paramount, Vaughn was forced to concede and Ottman was hired. On 13 December 2006 the *Smallville* fan site Krypton Fan included an interview with Ottman as part of its weekly podcast.[54] The interviewer's principal concern is the composer's work on the then recent release *Superman Returns*, but there is also some discussion of Ottman's upcoming film-scoring projects. In addition to *Fantastic Four: Rise of the Silver Surfer* and *The Invasion*, Ottman says "I've got, I think, a fantasy movie called *Stardust* that I'll be working on, but I'm not sure about that yet. And I think that comes out in July."[55] Ottman seems unsure about his involvement with *Stardust* at the time of the interview, but anecdotal evidence from various internet film-music forums indicates that he worked on the project in late 2006 and early 2007, and was due to record a complete score in February 2007. However, in the intervening period there were significant changes in the Paramount hierarchy that altered the landscape in which *Stardust* was being produced. Company president Gail Berman resigned her post on 10 January, a move that led to other dismissals and a significant restructuring of part of the corporation.[56] Dissatisfaction with Ottman's score led to Vaughn approaching his new bosses at Paramount regarding Eshkeri, and in late January 2007 he was officially brought onto *Stardust*, first as co-composer, and then as sole composer of the score.

The political situation that developed around the scoring of *Stardust* impacted on the sound of the film in several ways. According to Eshkeri, the temp track for *Stardust* included some cues from his back catalogue, the two demos that he wrote for Paramount, and material drawn from other films and libraries in line with standard industry practice.[57] The presence of so much of Eshkeri's music on the temp track placed Ottman at a disadvantage before he had even written a note, especially since the montage sequence aboard the Caspartine had been cut to fit Eshkeri's demo. The challenge of creating a score that Vaughn would find suitable despite not being the director's preferred composer was always going to be demanding, but having to compete with Eshkeri's material amplified the difficulty enormously. McLaughlin recalls that Vaughn placed Ottman "under a lot pressure and made him do the stuff really quickly and he didn't really give him a fair shot at it," so it is unsurprising that he spent less than three months as composer on the project.[58] The on-going disagreement regarding the appropriate composer led to varied musical interpretations of the film across the end of the production period and the start of post-production. On 21 July 2006, around two months before principal photography was completed, a blogger from the website *Aint it Cool News* was invited to Pinewood Studios to tour the set and watch some rough cuts. One such sequence was Tristan running to the wall to stop Yvaine from leaving Stormhold, which he reports as follows:

> As he [Tristan] went running to warn her [Yvaine], the music swelled, and I just had time to recognize *Starman* by David Bowie before the vocals kicked in. Honestly, that three and a half minutes was better than some films that are out now. The rough version of that footage made the hair on the back of my neck stand up. I hope that's some of what they show anyone who attends the *Stardust* panel today [at Comic-Con 2006]. Once you guys see it, I think it'll go a long way toward explaining the tone of this particular world.[59]

There are narrative connections between the Bowie track and the film—notably the idea that stars are people—and the use of this song created a distinct impression in the mind of the blogger regarding the look and sound of *Stardust*. Nevertheless, the Bowie track was excised and the final film soundtrack bears no trace of it. The theatrical trailer presents a rather different sound world for the film, featuring an eclectic mix of music for fantasy and animated adventures (by Thomas Newman, and John Powell and Harry Gregson-Williams respectively), orchestral black metal courtesy of the Norwegian group Dimmu Borgir and the Prague Philharmonic Orchestra, and library music from Two Steps From Hell and Future World Music, both companies that specialise in providing music for theatrical trailers and other associated filmic derivatives. The international trailer, which features a slightly different cut of the visuals, also includes music by another two composers who specialise in this sort of music, Andrew Jensen ("Dreamscape 6") and Robert Etoll ("Quest of Kings"). Table 3.1, below, shows the sources for the various musical excerpts used in the trailer.

It is unusual for a fantasy film to make use of such a large number of source materials,[60] and the confused musical voice of the trailer matches the somewhat misleading version of the film it portrays. Indeed, while it must be acknowledged that the trailer was created by an external company, it is heavily criticised on internet message boards for the way it presents the film, and is widely blamed (by fans as well as some critics) for the picture's lukewarm reception on release.

Table 3.1. Music used in the official theatrical trailer for *Stardust*

Time	Source	Comments
0.00–0.04	–	No sound over certification screen.
0.05–0.16	Two Steps From Hell, "Adventures of Enchantment" from the album *Volume One.*	Taken directly from the track, 0.04–0.15.
0.17–0.30	–	Held pitches with dialogue. No source track.
0.31–0.42	Thomas Newman, *Lemony Snicket's A Series of Unfortunate Events*, "Hurricane Herman."	Taken directly from the track, 0.29–0.40.
0.43	–	Silence.
0.44–1.02	Dimmu Borgir, "Eradication Instincts Defined" from the album *Death Cult Armageddon.*	0.00–0.22 of the track, slightly cut in the trailer to match cuts in the visual action.
1.03–1.22	John Powell and Harry Gregson-Williams, *Chicken Run*, "Into the Pie Machine."	0.27–0.38, then a direct cut to 1.00–1.08.
1.23–1.39	Future World Music/Armen Hambar, "Uprising" from the album *Epic Action—Volume 1.*	Material from 0.00–0.11 recut and repeated to match the pacing and cuts in the trailer.
1.40–1.45	–	Sound effects and dialogue.
1.46–2.05	Future World Music/Armen Hambar, "Uprising" from the album *Epic Action—Volume 1.*	Taken directly from the track, 0.36–0.55.
2.06–2.25	Future World Music/Armen Hambar, "Uprising End Ver 2" from the album *Epic Action—Volume 1.*	The entire 0.19 alternative ending to the "Uprising" track.

The various decisions taken by the production company resulted in *Stardust* having no coherent or consistent musical voice throughout its creation, despite the availability of a composer on the set. Accordingly, a number of musical and filmic influences can be determined in Eshkeri's score, which attempts to combine the elements of fantasy, romance, adventure, action and mild horror found in the narrative.

Stardust in Context

The story is very much a fantasy/mission movie along the lines of *The Princess Bride* or *Lord Of The Rings*, but with Gaiman's skewered reality laid on top of everything.[61]

While *The Princess Bride* is a specific (and widely acknowledged) model for *Stardust*, the creative team went to great lengths to distance their film from other fantasy features, particularly that listed in the above remark, *The Lord of the Rings*. Vaughn's strategy in this regard involved keeping the film as grounded as possible, by relating elements of the fantastical world to real life and trying to avoid replicating the look of Peter Jackson's trilogy. Many aspects of the world beyond the wall are based on existing models, designs and architecture—the witches' lair draws on the Palace of Versailles, and Primus's coach is based on the shape of a Hummer car—but adapted and recontextualized to make them seem "comfortable, but not too familiar."[62] There is also an attempt to underplay magic in *Stardust*, Vaughn wanting it to be viewed as an everyday activity on that side of the wall, "like paying a bill in our world,"[63] though surprisingly there is a specific musical texture often heard when magic appears in the film.

The sequence (Figure 3.1, below) is based around an augmented chord, drawing on the whole-tone scale that is often used to represent magic or mysticism in Western classical music. The orchestration was developed by the composer in collaboration with Robert Elhai, and Eshkeri recalls that it functioned as an orchestrational model that was employed throughout the score at points where magic features on-screen. However, this is an overly simplistic interpretation of the role of this musical effect. Although the "magic" texture accompanies the vast majority of small spells and enchantments, it is often absent at larger magical moments, such as Lamia's creation of the inn, and the duel between the witch queen and Ditchwater Sal that leads to the latter's death. The result of this is that Eshkeri's discerning placement of the material reflects Vaughn's desire to downplay the importance of magic. Although the music functions as a calling card for small-scale instances, larger, more dramatically-significant moments are accompanied by 'non-magical' music, exactly like key non-magical sequences.

Vaughn's approach to the individuality of *Stardust* was echoed by other members of his crew, though the team members were not ignorant of the difficulties they faced. Producer Lorenzo Di Bonaventura explains that "a lot of the story is told in very dramatic landscapes, and so like *Lord of the Rings* in particular, it has that tremendous backdrop in much of the movie,"[64] making sourcing appropriate locations for the film a significant challenge. Extensive research was undertaken to find appropriate natural landscapes that differed significantly from those found on Jackson's Middle Earth, the result of which was on-location shooting being carried out in Iceland, the Isle of Skye, the Brecon Beacons in Wales, and Cobham Common in Surrey. The CGI landscapes needed for the film were based on aerial photographs and map data also taken from the Isle of Skye, creating a striking and consistent backdrop for Stormhold that maintained the epic grandeur, but not the precise look of *The Lord of the Rings*.

Figure 3.1. *Stardust*'s "Magic" texture, bars 23–25 from 1M4 "Snowdrop"

However, the *Stardust* team could not reasonably sever all ties to the fantasy genre, and there are some elements of the visual construction of the film that owe a debt to *The Lord of the Rings*. This is doubtless unintentional, and ironically in some cases may actually have arisen as a result of the strategy of basing Stormhold on reality. Interviewed during the production process, Charles Vess offered this view of the visual appearance of the film:

> "They started with my work, and the film will have all the grace and the terror, but it will look different," he [Vess] admits. "The designers have gone into their own space, but they developed the same world, just slightly different viewpoints. For example, the exterior of Stormhold Mountain Inn looks like my paintings, but the interior is different."[65]

Vess asserts that his artwork was the source on which the film's castle was based, but following a backstage tour of the studio a reporter from *Aint it Cool News* observed that the building is "like Minas Morgul from *ROTK* [*The Lord of the Rings: Return of the King*], however with more historical England looking architecture."[66] The top of the citadel with its outer walls and tall central tower is indeed reminiscent of Minas Morgul, but the similarities with the land of Gondor run deeper. Designs and scale models of the Stormhold mountain produced by the film's art department show it as an all-black city enwrapped by a mountain that rises up from the ground to the citadel at the summit.[67] This is effectively an inversion of Gondor's multi-level capital, Minas Tirith, which is an all-white city wrapped around a central shard of mountain. Additionally, the final narrative purpose of both cities is the same: the location for the coronation of a new king (Tristan and Aragorn respectively). Production designer Gavin Bocquet remarks that when creating *Stardust* "you wanted to try and exclude it being *Harry Potter*, you wanted to exclude it being *Lord of the Rings*," and it is clear that the connections between Stormhold and Gondor are far from deliberate. However, it is also apparent that even when a conscious attempt is made to differentiate a contemporary fantasy film from *The Lord of the Rings* it is still extremely difficult, if not impossible, to remove all trace of its influence while remaining within the requirements and expectations of the genre.

Additional intertextual relations between the films are created through the voiceovers that appear in *Stardust*, the connection coming through the choice of narrator. The voice in question is that of Sir Ian McKellen, and although Jane Goldman asserts that "no-one comes near" him in terms of delivery, he brings associations with a number of other films to bear on *Stardust*.[68] Voiceovers are inherently problematic since they often provide the viewer with more information than is known by the characters, raising questions as to the authority and perspective on which the apparent facts are presented. In this case, since many film-goers will doubtless recognise the voice in *Stardust* as that of Sir Ian McKellen, additional questions are raised regarding whether this is the voice of the trustworthy Gandalf (*The Lord of the Rings*) the manipulative Magneto (*X-*

Men), or indeed any other of his multitude of previous roles. A connection to Gandalf is, perhaps, the most likely considering that *Stardust* is in the fantasy genre, and the film benefits from the authority afforded to the voiceover by this intertextual link. Whether intentional or otherwise, *Stardust* profits from viewers relating it to *The Lord of the Rings* in this way. The voiceovers are just a small part of the film's sonic environment, the most prominent component of which is Eshkeri's score. The music will be analysed, and then evaluated in the context of the post-*Lord of the Rings* era in Chapter 5, after the following consideration of its creation, development and realisation through the film-score production process.

4

CREATION AND PRODUCTION OF THE SCORE

The following chapter explores the processes and timelines of the score's creation so that the development of the music can be examined and understood. The vast majority of the *Stardust* score was composed, orchestrated and recorded between February and May 2007, though the first new idea for the score was formed much earlier, in late 2005. There are eighty-five cues plus the closing song by Take That, and it is therefore not possible to consider all of them in detail. Accordingly, the chapter proceeds by offering a rigorous critical evaluation of the score's timeline, drawing on specific cues to provide examples of the ways in which the production process impacted on the creation and development of the music. The investigation is conducted within the context of a new model of contemporary film-score production in the UK that provides a more comprehensive and true-to-life interpretation of the processes involved in creating a film score.

General Timeline of the Score

The musical score for a film is commonly composed exclusively within the post-production phase after completion of all principal photography, with the composer given the chance to view a 'rough cut' of the film. Composers will often read a script ahead of the rough cut viewing so that they can become better acquainted with the world of the film, the narrative and the characters, though there is every likelihood that the actuality of the picture will not tally entirely with the written text.[1] In order to appreciate the complexities of film-score production properly and interpret the interactions between the main processes of composition, orchestration and recording accurately, it is essential that these activities are not viewed as discrete and sequential. As will become clear, the composition, orchestration and recording of cues often overlapped on *Stardust*— notwithstanding the fact that all composition and orchestration was completed before the final recording session on 25 May 2007—and the version numbers of several cues bear testimony to the iterative nature of the whole creative process.

A non-linear conceptual model of film-score production is employed in this chapter to enable an accurate reading of the various overlapping timelines for individual cues.[2] The model was developed through consultation with composers and orchestrators active within the British film-music industry, and challenges a number of assumptions present in other representations and accounts of film-score production. Importantly, the model operates on three fundamental premises. Firstly, a film score is not produced *en masse* as a single artifact. Each cue may be created independently of all others, so there is unlikely to be a single pathway taken by 'a score' through the production process. Secondly, the various production activities (such as composition, orchestration and recording) are not discrete events, meaning that there is not a specific point at which (for instance) composition ends and orchestration starts, or when orchestration ends and recording starts. Related closely to this, the final underlying tenet of the model is that there is not a single, fixed order of processes through which a cue will progress. Individual cues may repeat or omit parts of production processes depending on their unique requirements, owing to the iterative nature of film-score composition.[3] As this author has observed elsewhere,

> while it seems clear that the process must begin with the engagement of a composer and be completed by final dubbing, the interim steps will not necessarily occur in the same strict order for every cue of every film [. . .] [There are] times in the process when composing, orchestrating and recording run in parallel. Similarly there are aspects of composition, orchestration and arrangement which take place within recording sessions.[4]

The model (see Figure 4.1, below) is a flow diagram, with decision points and arrows that enable each cue to take a non-linear pathway through the process. No attempt is made within the model to account for relative time periods or the importance of the different activities, and neither of these facets should be interpreted from it: the various boxes in the flow diagram vary in size only to allow the clear presentation of all necessary information. Importantly it is a model of processes, and not of people or roles. Accordingly, while the composer's involvement is not confined to the

"Conceptualizing and Composing" of a cue, should further conceptualization or composition be required after the composer's initial attempts the model enables a return to these activities later in the process. Similarly, changes made at recording sessions may involve minor edits to the parts ("Copying and Editing"), adjustments to the orchestration ("Orchestrating and Arranging"), recomposition or new composition of material ("Conceptualizing and Composing"), or even a complete restart owing to changes in the cutting of the film ("Spotting, Timings and Synchronization"). Whether or not these activities take place within or outside the session does not matter—the model allows the *processes* to be revisited without consideration of where, when or by whom they are undertaken.

Most of the activities included in the model can be traced back to other accounts of the film-score production process such as Karlin and Wright's *On the Track*, but there are three activities that require further explanation here.[5] "Mocking Up/Demoing" refers to the practice of scoring electronic demos for a MIDI or sample orchestra to create an aural impression of the finished cue. In the late 1990s and early twenty-first century this was commonly accomplished using Gigastudio software, though in the contemporary industry Native Instruments' Kontakt now holds the majority of the market share in this area of technology. An additional sub-flow chart exists within "Orchestrating and Arranging" owing to specific research into the role of the film-score orchestrator carried out alongside the creation and development of the model. The intricacies of this part of the process are not considered within this evaluation of *Stardust*, but the sub-flow chart is shown in Figure 4.1 since it is a constituent part of the model. The final term that appears in the model that cannot be found in Karlin and Wright's interpretation of the process is "Sweetening." This aspect of film-score production has been considered in Chapter 2 within the context of Eshkeri's working practices, and a full description of the activity can be found there (see Chapter 2, note 49).

The discussions that follow in this chapter use the model to construct and demonstrate the individual production timelines for several cues from *Stardust*. However, it should be remembered that gaps in the available data inevitably mean that it is not always possible to ascertain the dates and versions of cues precisely.

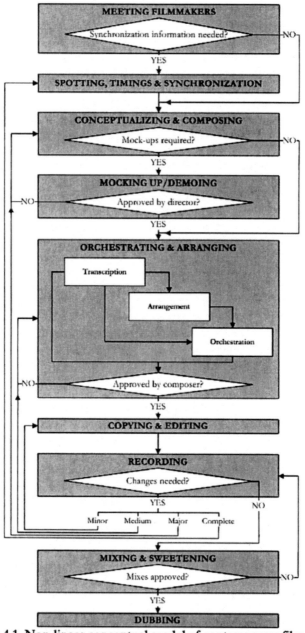

Figure 4.1. Non-linear conceptual model of contemporary film-score production in the UK[6]

The production process for Eshkeri's score is contextualized and interrogated within the framework of this model, enabling the creation of a composite picture of the development of the score. The following investigation also demonstrates the ways in which the production process impacted on the music, and establishes additional groundwork ahead of the analysis and reading of the score in Chapter 5. Importantly, although John Ottman's involvement with *Stardust* occurred during the period in which Eshkeri was working on ideas for the film (whether officially or unofficially), Eshkeri's score is the sole focus of this evaluation.

Ilan Eshkeri's *Stardust*

Early Ideas

Eshkeri's official employment on *Stardust* began in early 2007, though his involvement with the project began long before this. He recalls a telephone conversation with Vaughn that took place well before a film was even mooted, in which the director told him that he was thinking of writing a script and advised Eshkeri to read the book. Vaughn also visited Eshkeri at North Pole Studios in 2005, before shooting began and over two years prior to the film's release, at which time he was still writing the first draft of the script.[7] It was at this meeting that Vaughn first mentioned *Twinkle, Twinkle Little Star* as a possible musical source, as outlined in Chapter 2, and Eshkeri recalls "[doing] something there and then that became *Stardust's* first motif."[8]

When film production got underway in early 2006 Eshkeri read both the script and the original graphic novel, and as has already been noted, owing to his close relationship with Vaughn, Eshkeri spent a lot of time on set while *Stardust* was being shot. He also met with Neil Gaiman and Charles Vess to discuss "the characters, the world and the style of *Stardust*,"[9] and studied Vess's original drawings for the story. Eshkeri's engagement with the writers, and his presence on the set during the shooting of the film mark departures from 'normal' practice, and afforded him increased opportunities to engage with Vaughn's (and Gaiman's) vision of *Stardust*. He recalls writing music on set, notably the two demos requested by Paramount in July 2006. These pieces—the $\frac{6}{8}$ "Septimus" theme (orchestrated by Julian Kershaw), and a version of the "Pirate Montage" inspired by Vess's drawing *Flying Ship* (orchestrated by Robert Elhai)[10]— were the first full musical ideas composed for the picture, and both are present in some form in the final cut of the film.[11] In addition to demonstrating his capability to Paramount, Eshkeri's music also had value on the set, where it was sometimes used as unofficial mood music, recalling a similar practice from the silent era. In this regard, he remembers that

> Jason Flemyng [who played Primus] and Charlie Cox [Tristan] would come in and they'd be about to do some horse-riding scene and they'd be like "play that thing again [Septimus]" and they'd be like, "ok cool, I'm ready for it now" and then go back out [to shoot the scene].[12]

Robert Elhai's file archive from the project contains a compositional sketch for the "Pirate Montage" demo in the form of a Digital Performer file, which is dated 25 July 2006. This sketch demonstrates how well Eshkeri understood Vaughn's intentions for the scene, which had not even been shot at the time this music was composed.[13] The demo runs to 85 bars and lasts around 2.30 minutes, only diverging significantly from the final cue (written some nine months later) in the closing bars. There are small differences—the inclusion or omission of a $\frac{2}{4}$ bar, and minor changes to the melody's rhythmic profile for instance—but to a large extent the demo emphasizes the remarkable sense of clarity that Eshkeri had even during the early stages of scoring *Stardust*. His presence on the set, conversations with the original creative team, and interactions with the novel and drawings that had inspired Vaughn in the first place, cannot be overestimated here.

The final preliminary compositions written before the main body of scoring date from late January 2007, shortly after Eshkeri had been hired by Paramount. The composer sent two emails to Steve McLaughlin containing mocked-up mp3 files titled "Ruff *Stardust* Idea" and "Ruff *Stardust* idea v3," the latter of which is transcribed below (Figure 4.2). When considered as a whole the piece bears little relation to any cue from the film, but there are significant elements within this early sketch which take fuller form within the score.[14] Eshkeri sent Elhai a tentative idea for the witch material on 27 January, and like the "Ruff *Stardust* Idea v3," it is an amalgam of elements that are used in the final score rather than an early version of any particular cue. The material includes several features associated with Lamia and the witches—a driving triple-time bass line, shifting three-part chords and the interval of a tritone—but no indication of how they might be used in context.[15] The opening of the demo actually bears a striking resemblance to the start of 6M64 "Lamia Rides," though unsurprisingly the cue is considerably more refined in its use of the constituent "witch" elements, and it is clear that Eshkeri did not have this sequence in mind when he sent the file to Elhai.

A further mp3 file was sent by Eshkeri to McLaughlin on the evening of 28 January 2007. The demo is entitled "Love theme," and Eshkeri's email explains that it "plays against the bush and the mouse (slower than this demo),'' indicating its suitability for use in both 5M49 "Hedge Love" and 5M55 "Mouse Love."[17] The complete theme does not actually appear in the film, but it exists at the end of the composer's score in an orchestration by Kershaw, was recorded for the album,[18] and is heard in its entirety at the end of the fifth movement of the *Stardust* orchestral suite. As Eshkeri indicated to McLaughlin, elements from the love theme can be found in 5M49 "Hedge Love" and it also features in the closing parts of 7M76/77 "Coronation Parts 1 & 2," though it is not found in any version of 5M55 "Mouse Love."

Figure 4.2. Reduction of "Ruff Stardust Idea v3"[16]

As with most of the musical material for *Stardust*, the "Love theme" underwent a process of significant refinement across the period of composition, though the main thrust of the melodic idea was retained by Eshkeri throughout this process. Figure 4.3 shows the melody for the original and final versions of the "Love theme." The opening pair of phrases with the prominent arpeggio shape and I–IV–vi–V harmony are retained across the revisions to the theme (albeit with the entire piece transposed from F to D), and the harmonic profile of the following bars is retained despite small changes to the melody. The original and final versions only diverge significantly in the closing bars, where Eshkeri's first effort utilizes a ii–vi–IV–V chord pattern to enable a return to the tonic, and the final version introduces a flattened 7th in the melody (the C♮ in bar 12) to push the harmony towards the subdominant for a return of the theme.

Figure 4.3. Melody from the "Love theme" as played on piano by Eshkeri in January 2007 (top), and as found in the orchestral score dated 25 May 2007 (bottom)

The last demo from this first (extended) period of composition dates from 3 February, and is titled "*Stardust* theme 1M1." The track has a running time of 1:46 minutes, identical to that of "Ruff *Stardust* Idea v3," but rather than another hotchpotch of ideas, the new piece is a clear forebear of the final cue used in the film. Structurally it is virtually identical to 1M1, though the overall duration of the cue and some of the sections within it indicate that it was composed to a different cut of the film than was used in the theatrical release. Evidence for this, and of other ways in which changes to the film itself affected the work of Eshkeri and his team, can be found in the range of surviving archival materials from the film-score production process.

Music Production: February to May 2007

Timings and Videos

Music production assistant Christoph Bauschinger sent two sets of timings to Eshkeri at the end of February 2007. The documents are effectively spotting notes, and give the start, end and running times of the film's cues along with brief outlines of the visual action underscored by each piece of music, and the current version number of each reel of film. It is apparent from these sources that a lot of work took place in a very short space of time, since the first file was sent on 27 February, and the second, sent the following day, is labeled as version 4. Around half of the 77 listed cues show a change of duration from version 1 to version 4 of the notes, and one cue, 5M56, moves from the end of reel 5 to the start of reel 6 (becoming 6M56 in the process). The main reason for these changes appears to be that Bauschinger was working through new cuts of the film that had been delivered to Eshkeri and McLaughlin, and in his email to Eshkeri with the version 4 notes he indicates that further changes are likely since "the video to work on in reel 7 is cut 11, which is not yet on your drive."[19]

Table 4.1. Reel versions and the dates they were received by Eshkeri

Reel	Delivery 1		Delivery 2	
1	v10.0	15 February		
2	v10.0	9 February	v10.5	1 March
3	v9.0	9 February	v9.5	27 February
4	v9.0	13 February	v9.3	27 February
5	v10.0	8 February		
6	v11.0	15 February		
7	v10.0	15 February	v11.0	No later than 27 February

The data in Table 4.1 are drawn from emails sent by assistant editor James Winnifrith and first assistant editor Tamsin Jeffrey to Eshkeri between 15 and 27 February, as well as QuickTime video files made available to the author by Robert Elhai. Winnifrith's email details the (then) current versions of each reel of film, Jeffrey's informing the team that reel 7 has progressed to v11.0 owing to the inclusion of new special effects that have required a slight recutting of the visuals and resulted in a shortening of the reel's running time.[20] Each of the QuickTime videos has the version number and date of creation embedded within it, and although Elhai did not have complete video recordings for the whole film among his surviving materials, he was able to provide extracts from each of reels 1 to 6 that he was sent by Eshkeri on 22 March 2007.

Sketches and Scores

1M1 appears to have been the first proper cue sent to Elhai, on 13 March, before he received the associated QuickTime video, with the remaining MIDI demos fed to the orchestrators piece-meal over the following two months. The final cues, 5M55 "Mouse Love" and 7M75 "Coronation 2" (actually an early version of the whole coronation scene, 7M76/77 and 7M78 together) were delivered to Elhai on 14 May. It is clear from the dates of the mp3 demos and Digital Performer sketches sent from composer to orchestrator, the orchestrator's Finale files, and the PDF scores returned to the composer, that the composition and orchestration of the score overlapped considerably. Table 4.2 shows the dates on which the first mp3 and sketch files were sent by Eshkeri to one of his orchestrators and the first orchestrations and scores that they produced, in addition to dates in April and May that show the first (and in most cases only) occasion on which cues were recorded. Gaps in the table indicate that no documentary evidence survives for the missing information; cues are presented on alternate white and grey backgrounds to enable easy reading across the table.

Table 4.2. Dates of demos, sketches, orchestrations, scores, and first recording for *Stardust* cues

Cue	Title	Demo	Sketch	Orch.	Score	Rec.
1M1	Prologue	13/03/07	13/03/07	15/04/07	17/04/07	18/04/07
1M1A	Gatekeeper				10/04/07	18/04/07
1M2	Through the Wall	03/04/07	13/04/07	13/04/07	13/04/07	18/04/07
1M3	Market					19/04/07
1M3A	Market Smile				07/05/07	09/05/07
1M4[/6]	Snowdrop	30/03/07	30/03/07	02/04/07	02/04/07	18/04/07
1M6A	Tristan	03/04/07	09/04/07	18/04/07	18/04/07	19/04/07
1M7	Tristan's Failure				10/04/07	19/04/07
1M8	Victoria					19/04/07
2M10	Picnic				21/05/07	22/05/07
2M10A	To Stormhold	11/04/07	11/04/07	17/04/07	18/04/07	18/04/07
2M10AR	To Stormhold			18/04/07	19/04/07	-
2M11	Secundus Enters		07/04/07		10/04/07	-
2M11 Alt	Secundus Enters		07/04/07		11/04/07	10/05/07
2M12	Secundus Dies				10/04/07	18/04/07
2M12 Alt	Secundus Dies				17/05/07	25/05/07
2M13				10/04/07		-
2M14A Pt 1	Necklace					25/05/07
2M14A Pt 2	Necklace	18/04/07	19/04/07	19/04/07	19/04/07	18/04/07
2M14B	The Star Falls	07/04/07	12/04/07		13/04/07	18/04/07
2M15	Lamia's Youth	07/04/07	10/04/07	14/04/07	17/04/07	18/04/07
2M16A	Gatekeeper 2	15/04/07	15/04/07	19/04/07	18/04/07	19/04/07
2M16	Fight with Guard	02/04/07	02/04/07		13/04/07	20/04/07
2M17	The Crater				10/04/07	19/04/07
2M17R	The Crater	04/05/07	04/05/07		05/05/07	10/05/07
2M18	Una's Letter				10/04/07	19/04/07
2M18B	Candle Journey					19/04/07
2M19	Tristan and Yvaine in Crater				13/04/07	19/04/07
3M20R	Bishop's Chamber	17/04/07	25/04/07	29/04/07	26/04/07	09/05/07
3M21	Witches' Lair				10/04/07	18/04/07
3M22	Babylon Candle					19/04/07
3M23	Turned to a Goat				13/04/07	18/04/07
3M24	Pursuit Begins					20/04/07
3M25	Sal's Spell					19/04/07

Table 4.2. Dates of demos, sketches, orchestrations, scores, and first recording for *Stardust* cues (continued)

Cue	Title	Demo	Sketch	Orch.	Score	Rec.
3M26A	Septimus at Ocean				18/04/07	19/04/07
3M26B	Lamia Cliff				20/04/07	20/04/07
3M26B R	Lamia Cliff	19/04/07	30/04/07	01/05/07	01/05/07	09/05/07
3M26B RAlt	Lamia Cliff			01/05/07	01/05/07	09/05/07
3M26B RRR	Lamia Cliff	25/04/07	26/04/07	16/05/07	16/05/07	22/05/07
3M27	Unicorn Rescues Yvaine				13/04/07	18/04/07
3M28	Killing the Croc				10/04/07	19/04/07
3M29	Creating the Inn	07/04/07	09/04/07	20/04/07	20/04/07	20/04/07
3M29B	Unicorn Ride				21/05/07	22/05/07
3M30	Tristan's Dream				13/04/07	18/04/07
3M31	Coach Chase					25/05/07
3M31A	Primus				24/05/07	25/05/07
4M32	Lamia's Inn Part 1					19/04/07
4M33	Lamia's Inn Part 2			24/05/07	24/05/07	25/05/07
4M34	Lamia's Inn Part 3			25/05/07	25/05/07	25/05/07
4M35	Lightning Harvest	03/04/07	14/04/07	15/04/07	15/04/07	20/04/07
4M36	Tied Up in the Hold				10/04/07	-
4M36R	Tied Up in the Hold				17/04/07	19/04/07
4M36RR	Tied Up in the Hold				19/04/07	10/05/07
4M37	Septimus at Inn				10/04/07	18/04/07
4M37R	Septimus at Inn				15/05/07	22/05/07
4M38	Lamia in Coach				16/04/07	10/05/07
4M39	Hold Conversation				19/04/07	19/04/07
4M40	Magnificent Seven				16/04/07	20/04/07
4M41	Shakespeare (Falling Body)				13/04/07	20/04/07
5M43	Arrival at Ferdy's			21/05/07	21/05/07	22/05/07
5M44	Conversation				12/04/07	19/04/07
[5M45A]	Pirate Montage for Demo			25/07/06		
5M45A	Pirate Montage	19/04/07	20/04/07		20/04/07	20/04/07
5M45C	Waltz				08/05/07	10/05/07
5M45B	Pirate Waltz			20/04/07	01/05/07	09/05/07
5M46	Boat Landing				21/05/07	22/05/07
5M47	Captain Whispers				13/04/07	19/04/07
5M48	Wot a Freak!				08/05/07	25/05/07
5M49	Hedge Love				13/04/07	19/04/07
5M50	The Can Can				17/04/07	18/04/07
5M51	Milestone					19/04/07
5M52	Wet Septimus				10/04/07	18/04/07
5M53	Turned to a Mouse	11/04/07	11/04/07		18/04/07	19/04/07
5M54	Septimus Milestone				13/04/07	18/04/07
5M55	Mouse Love	09/05/07	10/05/07		10/05/07	10/05/07
5M55 Alt	Mouse Love			16/05/07	16/05/07	22/05/07
5M55 Alt R	Mouse Love	14/05/07	14/05/07	16/05/07	16/05/07	22/05/07
6M56	Turned from a Mouse				06/05/07	10/05/07
6M57	The Kiss	11/04/07			13/04/07	19/04/07
6M59	Witches Warn Lamia				30/04/07	10/05/07
6M60	Walk to Wall				04/05/07	09/05/07

Table 4.2. Dates of demos, sketches, orchestrations, scores, and first recording for *Stardust* cues (continued)

Cue	Title	Demo	Sketch	Orch.	Score	Rec.
6M61	Tristan Returns				06/05/07	10/05/07
6M62A	Tristan Runs to the Wall				21/05/07	22/05/07
6M62B	Yvaine Runs to the Wall				21/05/07	22/05/07
6M63	Sal Killed				09/05/07	22/05/07
6M63A	What Happened?			21/05/07	21/05/07	25/05/07
6M64	Lamia Rides	27/04/07	28/04/07	29/04/07	29/04/07	22/05/07
6M67	Outside Lamia Lair				04/05/07	09/05/07
7M68	Septimus Fights Witches [Elhai]	23/03/07	23/03/07		27/03/07	-
7M68	Septimus Fights Witches [Kershaw]	26/04/07	29/04/07		01/05/07	09/05/07
7M69	Voodoo Doll	03/05/07	04/05/07	06/05/07	06/05/07	09/05/07
7M70	Fat Witch Dies	30/04/07	01/05/07	04/05/07	03/05/07	09/05/07
7M71	Tristan Fights Lamia	04/05/07	04/05/07	08/05/07	08/05/07	09/05/07
7M72	Zombie Fight	29/04/07		07/05/07	07/05/07	09/05/07
7M72 Alt	Zombie Fight	08/05/07	12/05/07	12/05/07	18/05/07	22/05/07
7M72A	Chandeliers	08/05/07	08/05/07	10/05/07	08/05/07	09/05/07
7M72B	Lamia Fight 2	08/05/07	07/05/07	08/05/07	08/05/07	22/05/07
7M72C	Lamia Cries				09/05/07	09/05/07
7M73	Lamia Locks Doors	04/05/07	04/05/07	09/05/07	09/05/07	09/05/07
7M74	Shining [Toyne]				20/04/07	20/04/07
7M74	Shining [Elhai]	20/04/07	21/04/07	09/05/07	09/05/07	22/05/07
7M76–77	Coronation Pts 1&2	08/05/07	08/05/07		16/05/07	22/05/07
7M76–77R	Coronation Pts 1&2			24/05/07	24/05/07	25/05/07
7M78	Coronation Part 3			21/05/07	21/05/07	22/05/07

The summary information shown in Table 4.2 emphasizes the interplay between composition, orchestration and recording, showing clearly that these were not discrete phases of activity. Deeper analysis of the surviving archival files and documentation reveals the extent to which material was rewritten before it was sent to the orchestrator, and in some cases after that point. Some filenames include version numbers, and in several cases Eshkeri provided his orchestrators with updated demo and Digital Performer files after they had already started work on older versions of cues. As well as Vaughn's meticulous approach resulting in Eshkeri often having to produce several iterations of a cue before it was approved, it led directly to some longer cues being split into a number of smaller parts. Steve McLaughlin recalls that he

> broke the film down into a million different little tiny bits so that we could get it approved, because typically out of a big giant chase sequence you'd get 30 seconds that was good and then a minute that needed changes, and another 30 seconds. [. . .] Break it down into tiny little bits and then you'll get bits approved and other bits not approved, but at each meeting you'll get some work approved. Whereas if you

have a big nine-minute cue and the guy says he doesn't like the middle
bit, well it's not approved and psychologically it's a big problem. And
then of course at the end you join them back up again.[21]

This process led to cues such as 2M14 becoming three shorter cues—
2M14A Part 1, 2M14A Part 2, and 2M14B in this case—meaning that
Eshkeri could send these smaller cues to his orchestrators as they were
approved rather than having to gain Vaughn's approval for the complete
sequence. As shown in Table 4.2, the audio demo for 2M14B was delivered to Elhai on 7 April, the orchestrated score being returned to Eshkeri on 13 April, still five days before the composer sent 2M14A Part 2 to
the orchestrator. These two sections were recorded in mid-April, but the
first part of the sequence, 2M14A Part 1, was only recorded on the final
day in the studio in late May. Bearing in mind the limit on the amount of
material that can be used from a single three-hour recording session,[22] the
music team may have had scheduling problems had this music been kept
as a single cue, with the whole sequence having to be recorded on 25 May.

On a macro scale, the opening seven cues (1M1 to 1M6A) can be
viewed in the same light. The music runs continuously from the Paramount logo, through the prologue and Dunstan's adventure across the
wall, to the first appearance of the teenage Tristan as he heads for the
home of Victoria Forester, and apart from silences which are composed
into the various cues (notably the bars rest in 1M1A "Gatekeeper"), the
first break in the music comes nearly seven and a half minutes into the
film. Several of the cues within this extended sequence underwent revision before being sent to the orchestrators—1M1 reaching version 12 a
month after Eshkeri first gave a complete demo of the cue to Elhai—and
the final cues progressed piecemeal from composer to orchestrator over a
period of a fortnight. Although never documented as a single 7:22 minute
cue, these seven cues exemplify the point made by McLaughlin in the
above quote regarding getting small parts of a large sequence approved at
each meeting with the director.

V10	Title	Length Action	Start	End
1M4	Snowdrop	1:29 Tristran and Una Kiss thru to Map[23]	4:14	5:43
1M5	Map	0:47 Camera Pans across Map thru Guard delivering baby	5:42	6:32
1M6	Stardust Title	0:59 Cam Pans up to Title thru stone hitting window	6:32	7:29
1M6A	Humphrey Fight	0:24 Humphrey and Tristam fight With wooden swords[24]	8:03	8:27

**Figure 4.4. Extract from Bauschinger's Music Production Notes v4
showing cues 1M4 to 1M6A**

With this in mind, it is perhaps ironic that 1M4 "Snowdrop" is actually a
composite cue. The first mention of the cue is on Bauschinger's music
sheet of 27 February 2007, where it is listed as the first of three cues

(1M4, 1M5 and 1M6) that run directly into each other. Version 4 of the notes, produced the following day, gives the same details (Figure 4.4). No stand-alone music files survive from before this point, but the QuickTime video for the opening of reel 1 includes a version of all three of these cues. Even in this early version of the music it is clear that 1M4, 1M5 and 1M6 have been written as a composite cue, and there is a total absence of any files or records relating to 1M5 and 1M6 (beyond Bauschinger's notes). Later references to the material label it as 1M4/6, and all demo, orchestration and score versions of 1M4 are of the composite cue. Although substantively the same as the final cue, the version of 1M4 in the QuickTime video differs significantly in the bars accompanying the film's title. Instead of a thinned-down "magic" texture, the opening horn melody from 1M1 returns, though this was removed on Vaughn's instructions, as noted in Chapter 2. The title shot seems to have been particularly problematic for Vaughn; the corresponding visual effect—a pan up to the night sky where the word "Stardust" appears in the stars—also changed between this cut of the picture and the actual film, though the director remained unhappy with it even in the final release.[25]

Early Development of Cues

The video files, sketches, and orchestrated scores shed significant light on the early development of some cues, notably those from the first reel of the film. The following examination draws on archival sources to highlight some of the subtle and substantial changes in the score that occurred across the first two months of the music production process.

The first proper demo for 1M1 produced by Eshkeri dates from early February 2007, but it is not until the following month that a version of the cue of suitable duration was created. The audio demo and Digital Performer sketch sent to Elhai on 13 March are the same length as the final cue, though with small discrepancies in the content and internal structure. There is a fourteen-beat introduction of sustained upper-string chords, harp glissandi, and repeated patterns on celesta that precedes the entry of the solo French horn, and the sustained chords in the $\frac{6}{8}$ section that follows this melody are played by the strings. Bars 21–28 feature descending chromatic scales, leading directly into the first statement of the "Stormhold" theme on cor Anglais, switching to French horn for a repeat of the melody six bars later. The violins take the final iteration of the theme to bring the cue to a conclusion. This demo is synchronized with an unfinished cut of the visual footage in the QuickTime video Eshkeri sent to Elhai later that month, but based on the dates of the orchestrator's Finale files, it appears that Elhai did not work on this version of the cue at all.

One month later, Eshkeri sent a new audio demo and sketch to Elhai labeled "v12," that show some notable changes to the cue. The opening section of version 12 retains the instrumentation of the old demo, but removes one bar of $\frac{4}{4}$ before the horn solo resulting in the melody entering the texture sooner. These beats are reinserted immediately prior to the $\frac{6}{8}$ section, which now features a wordless female choir in place of the strings, and the succeeding chromatic scales are replaced with descending arpeggios. The opening iteration of the "Stormhold" theme is suppressed (following instructions from Vaughn), so the accompaniment is heard without any melody before the cor Anglais introduces the theme. These changes result in the demo matching the final cue very closely, as well as demonstrating how Eshkeri responded to the visual material when revising the music. The introduction of the female choir aligns with the first shot of a star shining in the night sky, establishing a connection that is retained throughout the score and forms a key part of Yvaine's musical characterization. Additionally, withholding the "Stormhold" melody ensures that it is first heard as the voiceover discusses Dunstan Thorn's letter enquiring about the presence of another world across the wall near his village, rather than under the words "the Royal Academy of Science in London, England." This subtle adaptation likewise serves to establish the narrative connotations of the theme, in this case linking it with the land across the wall, rather than England as was the case in the old version of the cue.

1M1 was recorded just five days after Elhai received the audio demo for version 12 from Eshkeri, and his surviving Finale files show how the orchestration was refined over several revisions of the cue in this short period. The first file appears to be a literal scoring of the audio demo, effectively tidying up the notation from Digital Performer and placing it within the score template for the *Stardust* 'A' orchestra.[26] Each of the next three files, all of which date from the following day, 16 April, show subtle developments of the orchestration. Elhai seems to have focused initially on the strings, with the most significant changes in the next two versions of the orchestration coming in these parts. The first introduces tremolos into most of the upper string parts at the start of the cue, and the second spreads the various arpeggio figures across the instruments of the string section. Wide-ranging passages for violin 2 and violin 1 are replaced with parts that dovetail across the section, leading to smoother textures and a greater range of instrumental timbres. Additional harmony is also included in this scoring, notably in bars 21–28, where the descending arpeggios (now in violin 2 and viola, and later cello) are supported by sustained notes in the first violins and the two flutes, as well as the female choir. The remaining two Finale files develop the woodwind, brass and percussion, doubling the vocal harmonies in the woodwind during the $\frac{6}{8}$ section and introducing different timbres to thicken and diversify the texture of the opening section. The woodwind and glockenspiel parts were adapted further in the final iteration of the orchestration, which also included subtle changes such as the shifting of the double bass notes from the strong to weak beats in bars 25–28. The PDF score for 1M1 dates from 17 April, and the orchestral parts were recorded at the first session, held the following day.

By contrast, the two cues that follow the opening, 1M1A and 1M2, are unchanged between the demos heard on the QuickTime video and music found in the final scores. Although only the PDF scores exist for these cues, the close similarities between the early sound and final notation indicate that although Eshkeri revisited some of the musical material for the opening section during March, other parts were left unchanged in this period. It is apparent that Vaughn was instrumental in the development of parts of the score, with changes made following discussions between the director and composer. In the QuickTime video, ethnic percussion provides the sole musical accompaniment to Dunstan's entry into the market, the orchestra only entering the texture as he sees Lady Una, who smiles at him. The cue that follows introduces both Sal's and Una's motifs as Dunstan interacts with them, but Vaughn felt it would be better to "play the market" rather than the characters, leading to significant changes to the music.[27]

Bauschinger's timing sheets show two cues in this scene, 1M3 "Market" and 1M3A "Market Smile," neither of which aligns with the cue heard on the QuickTime video, with music much more continuous through the scene as a result. While improvisatory percussion is still heard as Dunstan explores the market, it is accompanied by largely string-based harmonies that connect the music to the sound of the preceding cues. Sal's motif does not appear when she enters the shot, and as Una replaces her at the stall the score segues directly from 1M3 to 1M3A without a break. Una's melody is also missing, 1M3A "Market Smile" continuing with similar material to 1M3 in order to maintain the exotic atmosphere and "play the market" rather than the characters. 1M3A is unusual among the cues for this part of the film since it was not recorded in mid April, appearing instead on the schedule for 9 May. The reasons for this are unclear, since it is clearly present in Bauschinger's notes from the end of February, but its omission from Fraser's mid-April cue lists (considered in detail below) confirms that 1M3A had not even been composed at the point at which the other cues from reel 1 were being orchestrated and recorded.

The final part of the opening sequence comprises three further cues: 1M4, 1M6A, and 1M7. As outlined above, 1M4 "Snowdrop" is effectively a composite cue, a version of which is synchronized with the QuickTime video of reel 1. This music includes the horn melody from 1M1 under the title, and is therefore a version of the cue no higher than four, since the material sent from Eshkeri to Elhai on 29 March is labeled "v5" and includes the "magic" material in place of the horn. Additionally, version 5 differs in length significantly from that on the QuickTime video, ending with the pan through the film title rather than running until the stone hits the window as outlined in Bauschinger's notes (see Figure 4.4, above). The succeeding material is a separate cue, 1M6A "Tristan"—the original 1M6A "Humphrey Fight" was never written—and 1M7 is brought forward to cover the transition from the end of the fight through the scene change to Dunstan's kitchen. It is unclear at what stage these changes were made—certainly not before 28 February when Bauschinger prepared version 4 of the music production notes—or if version 5 of 1M4 is the first to finish with the title shot, but the revised length and cue breakdown were retained throughout the rest of the scoring process.

Elhai completed the orchestration of 1M4 "Snowdrop" v5 on 2 April. However, the Finale file shows that the cue was scored for the 'B' orchestra, a decision that was subsequently revised resulting in the music being re-orchestrated for the larger 'A' orchestra. Elhai produced a hybrid orchestration on 8 April, developing the original scoring through the addition of optional parts for second flute, second oboe, and tuba, and adding sweeping scalic passages for the flutes and first clarinet in the middle of the cue; the final orchestration, dating from 10 April, confirms the inclusion of these additional parts, resulting in the A orchestra line-up.

Progress Check: April 2007

Spreadsheets created by copyist Vic Fraser enable the overall progress of the score to be charted to a degree. Fraser's first "Cue Breakdown Sheet" dates from 11 April (Figure 4.5), and lists twelve cues plus an alternative version of 2M11 "Secundus Enters." The information includes a full breakdown of the instrumentation for each cue, though the orchestrators are only named at the top of the sheet and are not linked to specific cues at this point. Cross-referencing Fraser's list with Table 4.2 shows that with the exception of 7M68 "Septimus Fights Witches," which will be considered in more detail below, these were the only pieces of music for which full scores had been created, and had therefore reached the copyist, by 11 April. Although thirteen cues from a total of nearly ninety is not a particularly large proportion, Eshkeri had provided demos of twelve more to Elhai by this point, and Kershaw generated a further nine scores over the following two days, indicating that up to thirty-four cues were or were being orchestrated by this point.

"Stardust"   Comp: Ilan Eshkeri

Orch: J.Kershaw/R.Elhai

CUE	Tmp		Orch.		Title	STRINGS				WOODWIND				BRASS					Rhythm	Chos
						Vln	Vla	Vcl	Cro	Fl	Ob	Cl	Ban	Hns	Tpt	Tbn	Tba	Kbd	Harp	Tmp	Percussion	
1m1a			B		Gatekeeper	34	8	8	8		1	1	2									
1m4		A			Snowdrop	36	10	8	8	8	8	8	8	4	1	3	1	P		1	Cym/Marimba/W. Gong/Tam/BD	
1m7			C		Tristan's Failure	22	8	8	8	1	1	1			1					1			
2m11			B		Secundus Sisters	34	8	8	8	1	1	2	2	4	1	3				1		
2m11 AR			B		Secundus Sisters	34	8	8	8	1		2	2	4	1	3		1	1		Cym/BD	
2m12			B		Secundus Dies	34	8	8	8	1	1	2	2	4	1	3		C	1	1	BD/Cym/Glock	
2m17			C		The Crater	22	8	8	8	1				1				C	1	1		Y
2m18			C		Une's Letter	22	8	8	8	1	1	1						C	1	1		
3m21			B		Witches' Lair	34	8	8	8		1	2	2	4	1	3				1	Cym/BD/Tam Tam	
3m28			B		Killing The Croc	34	8	8	8	1	1	3	2	3	1	3				1	Cym/BD/Tam Tam	
4m34			C		Tied Up In The Hold	22	8	8	8	1	1			1				C	1			
4M37			B		Septimus At Inn	34	8	8	8	1	1	2	2	4	1	3		C		1	Cym	
5m5E			B		Wet Septimus	34	8	8	8		1	2	2	4		3				1	Cym	

Figure 4.5. Vic Fraser's *Stardust* cue breakdown from 11 April 2007

A second list was circulated by the copyist on 20 April (Figure 4.6, below), showing a marked progression in the state of the project. With fifty-four cues listed (plus 2M11 Alt), more than four times the number on the previous list, it is clear that a significant amount of work took place in the nine days between the distribution of each of these lists.[28] It is also apparent that some sections of the score were much closer to completion than others, as summarized in Table 4.3, below.

Table 4.3. Cues missing from Fraser's list of 20 April 2007[29]

Reel	Total Cues	Number Missing	Missing Cues
1	9	1	1M3A
2	16	2	2M10, 2M12 Alt
3	15	3	3M29B, 3M31, 3M31A
4	10	2	4M33, 4M34
5	15	6	5M43, 5M45B, 5M45C, 5M46, 5M48, 5M55
6	11	9	6M59, 6M60, 6M61, 6M62A, 6M62B, 6M63, 6M63A, 6M64, 6M67
7	12	11	7M68, 7M69, 7M70, 7M71, 7M72, 7M72A, 7M72B, 7M72C, 7M73, 7M76/77, 7M78

The missing cues include two extended sections—two parts of each of the Lamia's Inn scene from reel 4 and the pirate montage from reel 5—and the vast majority of reels 6 and 7. The omissions indicate that Eshkeri was partially restricted when choosing which cues to work on despite principal photography being completed four months before he was officially brought onto *Stardust*. Difficulties in the filming of some scenes, notably that in Lamia's Inn for which Vaughn was never able to shoot with all four of the featured principals at the same time,[30] and changes to the edit forced by the inclusion of CGI and special effects will both have delayed the availability of footage, preventing the music team from working on those parts of the film earlier in the process.

"STARDUST"

Comp: Ilan Eshkeri

Orch: J.Kershaw/R.Elhal/J.Toyne

Cue	Time	Orch.				Title	STRINGS Vln	Vla	Vcl	Cbs	WOODWIND Fl	Ob	Cl	Bsn	BRASS Hns	Tpt	Tbn	Tba	Rhythm K/Bd	Harp	Timp	Percussion	Chos	
1m1		A			BE	Prologue	26	10	8	6	2	2	2	2	6	2	4	1	C/P	1	1	Glock/Cym/Tam/W.Gong/Marimba		
1m1a			B		JK	Gatekeeper	24	8	8	6		1	1	2										
1m2			B		BE	Through the Wall	24	8	8	6	1	1	2	2	4	1	3		P	1	1	Wind Gn/Trgl/Cym		
1m3		A	B			Market	24	10	8	6	1	1	1	1	3				C	1	1	Cym/BD		
1m4		A			BE	Snowdrop	26	10	8	6	2	2	2	2	4	1	3	1	P	1	1	Cym/Marimba/W.Gong/Tam Tam/BD		
1m5a				C		Tristan	22	8	8	4			1							1				
1m7				C	JK	Tristan's Failure	22	8	8	4	1	1	1		1					1				
1m8				C		Victoria	22	8	8	4			1											
2m10a r																								
2m11			B		JK	Secundus Enters	24	8	8	6	1	1	2	2	4	1	3				1			
2m11 Alt			B		JT	Secundus Enters	24	8	8	6	1		2	2	4	1	3		1	1		Cym/SD		
2m12			B		JK	Secundus Dies	24	8	8	6	1	1	2	2	4	1	3		C	1	1	BD/Cym/Glock		
2m14a pt.1		A	B			The Necklace Pt.1	26	10	8	6					4	1	3	1			1	BD		
2m14a pt.2		A	B			The Necklace Pt.2	26	10	8	6	1	1	2	2	4	1	3		P	1	1	BD/W.Gong		
2m14b		A			BE	Star Falls	26	10	8	6	2	2	2	2	6	2	4	1	P/C	1	1	Trgl/BD/Tam/Mar/Chimes/Glock/W.Gn	V	
2m15			B		BE	Lamia's Youth	24	8	8	6	1	1	2	2	4	1	3		P/C	1	1	Mar/W.gong/BD/Cym/Tam/Chimes		
2m15a						Lamia's Youth Pt.1			8	6			1	1			3			1	1			
2m16		A			BE	Fight With Guard	26	10	8	6	2	2	2	2	6	2	3	1	P	1	1	Cym/BD/Trgl/Mar/Glock/Piatti		
2m16a r																								
2m17				C	JK	The Crater	22	8	8	4	1				1				C	1	1		V	
2m18				C	JK	Una's Letter	22	8	8	4	1	1	1						C	1	1			
2m18b						Candle Journey																		
2m19				C	JK	Tristan & Yvaine In Crater	22	8	8	4	1	1	1		1				C	1	1	BD/Tam Tam/Cym		
3m20		A				Bishop's Chamber	26	10	8	6	2	2	2	2	6	2	4	1	P	1	1	Cym/Tam/GC/BD/		
3m21			B		JK	Witches' Lair	24	8	8	6		1	2	2	4	1	3				1	Cym/BD/Tam Tam		
3m22																								
3m23			B		JK	Turned To A Goat	24	8	8	6	1	1	2	2	4		3			1	1	Tam Tam/BD		
3m24		A			JK	Pursuit Begins	26	10	8	6	2	2	2	2	6	2	4	1		1	1	Cym/BD/Tam Tam		
3m25																								
3m26a																								
3m26b		A				Lamia Cliff	26	10	8	6	2	2	2	2	6	2	4	1	P	1	1	Tam/BD/Cym		
3m27			B		JK	Unicorn Rescues Yvaine	24	8	8	6	1		1	1	4		3		C	1	1	BD/Cym		
3m28			B		JK	Killing The Croc	24	8	8	6	1	1	2	2	4	1	3				1	Cym/BD/Tam Tam		
3m29		A				Creating The Inn	26	10	8	6	2	2	2	2	6	2	4	1	P	1	1	Cym/BD/Tam Tam		
3m30			B		JK	Tristan's Dream	24	8	8	6	1	1	2	2	4	1	3		C	1	1	Cym/BD/Tam Tam		
4m32			B		NI	Lamia's In Pt.1	24	8	8	6	1	1	2	2	4	1	3		C	1	1	GC/Bs Xylo/Cym		
4m35		A			BE	Harvest Lightning	26	10	8	6	2	2	2	2	6	2	3	1	P	1	1	Tam Tam/BD/Mar		
4m36rr				C	JK	Tied Up In The Hold	22	8	8	4	1	1							C	1				
4M37			B		JK	Septimus At Inn	24	8	8	6	1	1	2	2	4	1	3		C		1	Cym		
4m38		A			JK	Lamia In Coach	26	10	8	6	2	2	2	2	6	2	4	1		1	1	Cym/BD/Tam Tam		
4m39																								
4m40		A			JK	Magnificent Seven	26	10	8	6	2	2	2	2	6	2	4	1		1	1	Cym/BD/Tam Tam		
4m41		A			JK	Shakespear (Falling Body)	26	8	8	6	2	2	2	2	6	2	4	1			1	Cym/BD/Tam Tam		
5m44			B		JT	Conversation	24	8	8	6	1	1	2	2					C	1	1			
5m45a		A				Pirate Montage	26	10	8	6	2	2	2	2	6	2	4	1	P	1	1	Cym/BD/W.Gng/Tam/Glock		
5m47			B		JT	Captain Whispers	24	8	8	6	1	1	2	2						1	1	BD		
5m49			B		JK	Hedge Love	24	8	8	6	1	1	2	2	4		3		C	1	1			
5m50		A			JK	The Can Can	26	10	8	6	2	2	2	2	6	2	4	1			1	Trgl/Piatti/BD		
5m51																								
5m52			B		JK	Wet Septimus	24	8	8	6			1	2	4		3				1	Cym		
5m53 rev																								
6m54			B		JK	Septimus Milestone	24	8	8	6			2	2	4		3				1	BD		
6m56																								
6m57			B		JK	The Kiss	24	8	8	6	1	1	1		1	1			C	1	1			
7m7a						Shining																		

Figure 4.6. Vic Fraser's *Stardust* cue breakdown from 20 April 2007

The only other cue with a score dating from 11 April or earlier is 7M68, which is missing from Fraser's list. Eshkeri provided audio demos and sketches to Elhai on both 23 and 27 March, Elhai producing an orchestral score for the cue on the latter date, but this seems not to have been passed to Fraser. The archival materials show that Eshkeri composed a new version of the cue, which was orchestrated by Kershaw in late April for the smaller 'B' orchestra, and it is this music that appears in the final film. It seems likely that the decision was taken to make substantial changes to the cue after Elhai had completed his orchestration, but in advance of Fraser preparing his initial cue list, resulting in the omission of 7M68 from both sets of lists even though materials exist that predate them. Indeed, while Fraser's documents offer significant information about the progress of the score in mid April 2007, it must be remembered that they are based entirely on the cues that had been passed to him by that stage, and do not account for those being composed or orchestrated at that point.

Recording Plans and Sessions

The proposed recording schedule for *Stardust* is elucidated in an email of 12 March 2007 sent from Steve McLaughlin to Randy Spendlove, then executive vice president of music and creative affairs at Paramount. In the message McLaughlin thanks Spendlove for visiting the studio to hear some demos, going on to say,

> We spoke briefly about the orchestra recording schedule—here's what I anticipate. I'm expecting to record about 70–80% of the score in three or four days in the week of 16 April. I'm also holding time on the 7th and 8th of May to complete the recording.[31]

Documentation from the score-production process confirms that studio sessions took place on 18–20 April, and a second round of recording was done slightly after McLaughlin anticipated, on 9–10 May. The orchestral components of forty-eight cues were recorded in April, with a further twenty-two orchestral cues captured in early May alongside ten re-recordings of cues from the April sessions, and vocal components for all ten cues that feature the female choir. McLaughlin's estimate was optimistic, with nearly 20% of the score still to be recorded on completion of these sessions, but given the delays suffered by the music team, notably with regard to reel 7 of the film, this is not surprising. Additional sessions were held at Abbey Road on the afternoon and early evening of 22 May at which most of the remaining cues were recorded (Take That were also at

Abbey Road to record *Rule the World* on that afternoon), with a final session held at Air Lyndhurst Studios on 25 May.[32]

Schedules for the April sessions were created by Daryl Kell and distributed around the music team, the documents listing the cues to be recorded at each session and the proposed recording order. They also show how rapidly plans were changed, since the session timings on Kell's schedules do not match those on an invoice from Andy Brown dated 13 April. Brown's invoice, which details the musicians required and payment rates for each call over the three days of recording, accounts for a four-hour and a three-hour session on each day, but in the event all sessions were three hours apart from Thursday afternoon, which extended to four.

Documentation for the sessions in May not only shows the cues to be recorded, but also gives brief notes on the status of each cue in the days leading up to the sessions, and the orchestrator's initials. Comments indicate that some cues required major or minor fixes indicating they were still with the composer, some were with the orchestrator (shown as "BE has it" or "JK has it"), and others were "at Copyist." In a couple of instances cues are shown with the comment "Needs approved MV," meaning that Vaughn had not yet cleared the music for inclusion in the film. The director was present at the recording sessions and maintained an active role in determining the sound of the film. Detailed ProTools notes kept by recording engineer Richard Lancaster provide a breakdown of each take of each cue at the sessions at Abbey Road on 9 and 10 May. In addition to specifying which musicians and sections of music were recorded in each take, the notes give information on the strengths and weaknesses for several takes for each cue, with comments such as "good MV" and "MV still not happy" emphasizing the director's continued involvement in the process. The details for 3M20R "Bishop's Chamber" are shown in Figure 4.7, below, and show the takes for each constituent part of the cue—strings, trumpet, and everything else—as well as the comedy (misspelled as "comdey") ending that is not marked in the orchestral score but was added during the session.

McLaughlin's general approach at the sessions was to mix the music live, but after a tutti rehearsal of a cue the orchestra was often split into instrumental groups so that balanced stems could be obtained.[33] Following a session, McLaughlin and Eshkeri listened to the stems at their own North Pole Studio, choosing the best takes and adjusting the mix as required. McLaughlin noted any stems that required remixing, and was able to adjust the internal balances at British Grove studio ahead of returning to North Pole to complete the mixing process. This procedure took place following each set of recording sessions, even though Eshkeri was still composing cues throughout April and early May, meaning that some cues may have been ready to be given to Daryl Kell for inclusion in the film before others had even been passed to the orchestrator.

Stardust ProTools Notes

Prod: Ben Eshkeri | Eng: Steve McLaughlin | Date: 9/5/2007 | Assistant Engineer: Jake Jackson

Operating System: 10.4.8
Software Version: 7.3.1
AD/DA Converters: 192

air

Title/Cue	Take	Playlist	Group	cp	Master	Comments	EDIT NOTES/Playlist info	Master Playlist
3m20R	1	1	orch	cp				
	2	2	orch	cp				
	3	3	orch	cp				
	4	4	orch	cp		adding accents everywhere - n14		
	5	5	strings	cp	strings		strings only	
	6	6	rest -	cp	rest -		the rest minus tpt and ww mexican moment	
	7	7	orch	pu	comdey ending	wild rehearsal	comedy ending	
	8	8	orch	pu		to tape		
	9	9	orch	pu		longer ending		
	10	10	orch	pu		no getting it		
	11	11	tpt	pu				
	12	12	tpt	pu				
	13	13	tpt	pu		connected notes and long end - good MV		
	14	14	tpt	pu		too big band		
	15	15	tpt	pu		good		
	16	16	tpt	pu	m	more accent on first note		

Figure 4.7. Extract from Richard Lancaster's *Stardust* ProTools notes from the sessions on 9–10 May

The *Stardust* Film-Score Production Process

As the above discussion has shown, composition, orchestration and recording overlapped significantly across much of the music-production period. While it is apparent that there were times between March and May 2007 when each of these processes took prominence, it is clear that they were not discrete phases of activity, and that they were carried out on a cue-by-cue basis. Some cues appear to have passed through the film-score production process in a relatively straightforward manner, but others were subjected to significant revisions, in some cases even after orchestration. Four versions of 3M26B "Lamia Cliff," three variants on 4M36 "Tied Up in the Hold" and 5M55 "Mouse Love," and two forms of several further cues were orchestrated and recorded, while in other cases cues were rejected by the director and adapted by the composer on multiple occasions. At least one cue in each reel reached a version number in double figures before it was finally approved by Vaughn, and even then it often took several takes in the recording sessions to capture a sound that also met with approval. The roles of the key members of Eshkeri's team—McLaughlin, Elhai, Fraser, Brown, and for this project, Kershaw and Kell—are also apparent, though they vary throughout the process.

The interactions between composition, orchestration and recording on *Stardust* can be most clearly summarized by drawing on the conceptual model of film-score production presented at the start of this chapter (see Figure 4.1, above). By applying the model individually to each of the film's cues it is possible to explore and clarify the ways in which these processes interacted, and the score was created, developed and realized. The model is applied to a small number of cues in Figure 4.8, overleaf, providing a snapshot of part of the *Stardust* film-score production process. Most activities are abbreviated for reasons of space—column widths and row heights vary for the same reason—but can be related directly back to those in Figure 4.1 (C&C is Conceptualizing and Composing, M/D is Mocking Up/Demoing, and so on).

Applying the model retrospectively can be difficult and is not always possible, since there is often insufficient documentation to produce a detailed timeline for every cue in a score.[34] However, the cues included in Figure 4.8 emphasize the overlaps between the various different activities that occurred across the whole of the score-production period. In addition to marking the various production processes, significant transformations such as the creation of an alternative version (Alt), the move to a revision (R), or a change in performing ensemble ('A' Orch, 'B' Orch), are also included where such information still exists. This supplementary information enables the processes to be evaluated in greater depth, while also providing an insight into the often subtle changes that occur during the creation of a score.

Despite some significant differences in timelines of the various cues, Eshkeri always retained a clear impression of the musical structure and narrative connections embedded within the score. The final chapter undertakes a close analysis of the principal thematic ideas and relationships in the music for *Stardust*, leading to a reading of Eshkeri's music as a contemporary fantasy score.

Date	1M1		1M4		3M26B			5M45A	
Apr 06	*Meeting Filmmakers (Unofficial)*								
Jul 06								C&C / O&A	M/D
Sept 06								O&A	
Jan 07	*Meeting Filmmakers (Official)*								
3–14/2	C&C	M/D							
15–26/2			C&C	M/D	C&C (as 3M26)	M/D (as 3M26)			
27–28/2	*Spotting, Timings & Synchronization*								
1–22/3	C&C	M/D	C&C	M/D	C&C (as 3M26B)	M/D (as 3M26B)		C&C	M/D
23–28/3									
29/3–2/4			O&A ('B' Orch)	C&E ('B' Orch)					
3–10/4			O&A ('A' Orch)	C&E ('A' Orch)					
11–15/4									
16–17/4	O&A	C&E							
18–20/4	Rec	M&S	Rec	M&S				O&A / Rec	C&E / M&S
25–30/4									
1–3/5	(activities below are for vocals)				O&A (3M26BR, Alt R)				
4–6/5	O&A / Rec	C&E / M&S	O&A / Rec	C&E / M&S	C&C (Alt)	M/D (Alt)	C&E (R)		
7–8/5									
9–10/5							Rec (R) / M&S (R)		
11–15/5					C&C (Alt RRR)	M/D (Alt RRR)			
16–21/5					O&A (Alt RRR)	C&E (Alt RRR)			
22/5					Rec (Alt RRR)	M&S (Alt RRR)			
23–24/5									
25/5					Rec (Alt RRR)	M&S (Alt RRR)			
May/ Jun 07	*Dubbing*								

Figure 4.8. Part of the *Stardust* film-score production process—several models in parallel

5M55		7M68		7M72				7M76/77		Date
Meeting Filmmakers (Unofficial)										Apr 06
										Jul 06
										Sept 06
Meeting Filmmakers (Official)										Jan 07
										3–14/2
										15–26/2
Spotting, Timings & Synchronization										27–28/2
										1–22/3
		C&C	M/D							23–28/3
		O&A								
										29/3–2/4
										3–10/4
										11–15/4
										16–17/4
										18–20/4
C&C	M/D	C&C	M/D							25–30/4
		O&A		C&C		M/D				1–3/5
		C&E						C&C	M/D	4–6/5
				O&A (72)	C&E (72)	C&C (Alt)	M/D (Alt)			7–8/5
		Rec	M&S	Rec (72)		M&S (72)				9–10/5
O&A	C&E									
C&C (Alt)	M/D (Alt)			C&C (Alt)		M/D (Alt)				11–15/5
				O&A (Alt)						
O&A (Alt)	C&E (Alt)			O&A (Alt RRR)		C&E (Alt RRR)				16–21/5
								O&A	C&E	
Rec (Alt)	M&S (Alt)			Rec (Alt RRR)		M&S (Alt RRR)		Rec	M&S	22/5
				C&C (Insert)	O&A (Insert)	C&E (Insert)		O&A (R)	C&E (R)	23–24/5
				Rec (Insert)		M&S (Insert)		Rec (R)	M&S (R)	25/5
Dubbing										May/ Jun 07

Figure 4.8. Part of the *Stardust* film-score production process— several models in parallel (continued)

5

ANALYSIS AND READINGS OF THE SCORE

Eshkeri's music for *Stardust* is highly thematic and makes use of leitmotif in a filmic if not entirely in a Wagnerian sense. Resonances of Shore's epic scores can be detected in the music for the vast majority of recent fantasy films, but in its construction Eshkeri's score perhaps has more in common with John Williams's music for *Star Wars*, arguably the model for all large orchestral scores written since the end of the studio era.[1] In her consideration of leitmotif in the *Star Wars* films, Irena Paulus demonstrates that Williams goes further than relating themes to characters, creating a Wagnerian "web of leitmotifs."[2] She asserts that all of the thematic ideas linked to 'good' characters can be related back to Williams's "Force" theme, which functions as a musical nucleus for all of the leitmotivic material for those on that side of the battle. The leitmotifs for most of the 'good' characters in *Stardust* can similarly be traced back to a single source theme, but unlike *Star Wars* the source is not actually present in the film itself. The 'evil' leitmotifs can be similarly clustered, and although there is no overarching musical relationship that binds these two families of leitmotifs, there are nonetheless connections that link them together and add coherence to the score.

This analysis proceeds by considering the good and evil leitmotifs in turn, detailing the influences on and construction of the individual themes in each group, evaluating their relationships, and showing how they are used and developed within the context of the filmic narrative. Following this, connections across the wider score are explored, and the musical soundscape as a whole is considered in the light of conventions for and requirements of fantasy film scores in the contemporary industry. Where they are not explicit in the discussion, cue numbers for *Stardust* are given in brackets for clarity.

'Good' Characters

There are a number of 'good' characters in *Stardust*, those who may have been associated with the Fellowship of the Castle in Gaiman's book, and generally operate in ways that assist or benefit Tristan and Yvaine. In addition to the protagonists, this group includes Captain Shakespeare and the pirates, and Lady Una. The entire land of Stormhold may also be considered in this collection, especially considering Alice Curry's assertion that Yvaine, as "a daughter of the moon and therefore an entirely natural being," can be seen as representative of the whole of the fantasy realm.[3]

Tristan

First seen briefly as a baby, Tristan is properly introduced as a seventeen-year old (1M6A) to the sound of a cor Anglais melody based around a major arpeggio (Figure 5.1). The instrumentation of the opening phrase evokes pastoral associations borne out of similar, prominent single-reed melodies in classical works such as Beethoven's Sixth Symphony, and the overture to Rossini's *Guilliame Tell*, and reflects the character's background in rural Wall. The second phrase is presented on French horn, implying a more majestic character, but a short rest between melodic phrases creates the sense that the horn simply answers the cor Anglais rather than asking further questions. This limits the potential of the music (and Tristan) at this stage in the proceedings, though the horn is heard as the voiceover discusses Tristan's development from a boy to a man, subtly hinting at his possible future.

Figure 5.1. Tristan's theme

The opening four notes form the "Tristan" leitmotif, the principal melodic link to the various derivations of Tristan's theme that occur through the score, but there is also a second short motif that gives rise to another recurring theme. The sixth and eighth bars of Tristan's melody each contain four-note descending lines, and this short phrase forms the basis of the "Tristan's Failure" leitmotif (Figure 5.2). The shape of the motif can be interpreted as an isomorphic 'sigh,' and unsurprisingly it is used at moments when Tristan meets with disappointment. Its first appearance is in 1M7 "Tristan's Failure," the cue immediately following the first presentation of Tristan's theme, when he is humiliated by Humphrey in front of Victoria and her friends. It returns when he revisits the scene of this embarrassment to ask Victoria to join him for a picnic (2M10) and she appears to rebuff him, but disappears for the middle part of the cue with her subsequent appearance at his side. However, it is heard again at the end of the scene when Tristan's rather unromantic depiction of bringing Victoria back the head of a polar bear as a gift results in him losing the opportunity to kiss her.

Figure 5.2. "Tristan's Failure"

Both of Tristan's leitmotifs are heard as he tries to persuade the guard to allow him to cross the wall in order to start his quest for the star (2M16A R). Tristan's melody underscores his approach to the guard, but Eshkeri inserts some silence into the middle of the phrase so that when the guard mistakes Tristan for his father the dialogue is unaccompanied. Tristan's theme returns as he announces himself ("no, it's Tristan actually"), the dialogue serving the dual purpose of identifying Tristan to the guard and reaffirming to the audience the connection between the music and the character. The cue closes with the final instance of the "Tristan's Failure" leitmotif, heard as Tristan starts to return home after the guard has reiterated his stance that no-one is allowed to cross the wall. In this instance, however, the cue matches the visual action but not the character's intentions, since Tristan dashes towards the gap in the wall as soon as the guard turns his back, exactly as his father did at the start of the film, seventeen years earlier. Tristan is unsuccessful however, the guard (who we later learn is ninety-two years old) having apparently become a master of the martial arts since he was duped by Dunstan. The "Tristan's Failure" leitmotif is not used in this cue (2M16),[4] possibly because the physical defeat far outweighs any emotional failure felt by the character, and possibly because its mournfulness would play against the comedic nature of the scene. When Tristan's adventure does finally get underway it is heralded by his leitmotif (2M18B), the use of French horn rather than cor Anglais reinforcing the narrative premise that he is about to leave the pastoral comforts of Wall and begin what will be a rite of passage.

Much later in the film, the consecutive cues 6M60 "Walk to Wall" and 6M61 "Tristan Returns" demonstrate Eshkeri's subtle use of Tristan's leitmotif to mystify and clarify his character and intentions. 6M60 accompanies a complex scene that opens with Tristan and Yvaine in a bedroom at the Slaughtered Prince Inn on the Stormhold side of the wall, and

proceeds to cross cut between the two characters as they make their independent walks towards the village of Wall. The cue includes sets of oscillating thirds in the accompaniment, sometimes major and sometimes minor, creating an air of ambiguity that calls into question Tristan's actions
and motivations as he leaves Yvaine asleep and embarks for Wall. Rhythmic disruption created by simultaneous use of regular and triplet quavers
increases the sense of unease, and points where the rhythmic movement
ceases only serve to amplify the effect when they return. Eshkeri places
fragments of several different melodies over this unsteady texture, one of
which is based on Tristan's leitmotif. However, it is presented in a minor
key and, for the only time in the score, without its characteristic two-note
anacrusis (see Figure 5.3).

**Figure 5.3. Bars 19–22 of 6M60 "Walk to Wall" showing the melody
based on Tristan's leitmotif without its anacrusis, and the rhythmically and harmonically restless accompaniment**

The scene witnesses Tristan leave an unintentionally cryptic message for
Yvaine, the innkeeper informing her that "he's gone to see Victoria, because he's sorry but he's found his true love, and he wants to spend the
rest of his life with her."[5] Though Tristan's intention is to tell Victoria that
he no longer wishes to marry her, Yvaine misinterprets his message as one
of goodbye, thinking that he has left her to return to Wall. His intentions

are also unclear to the viewer, and Eshkeri's manipulation of Tristan's leitmotif enhances the ambiguity of the scene.

Tristan's leitmotif is stated more clearly in the following cue, 6M61 (see Figure 5.4, below). He initially picks up a stone to throw at Victoria's window, as he did the last time he approached her on the evening he promised to find the star, before deciding instead to knock on her front door. His maturity is reflected in his theme, the rhythmic values for which are doubled from the original version; it is unhurried and more confident. However, the leitmotif does not accompany the moment Tristan's new attitude towards Victoria is made clear. Instead, Eshkeri quotes a short passage from part of Tchaikovsky's *Romeo and Juliet Fantasy Overture* to add romantic overtones to Victoria finally consenting to kiss him, but the music misleads the viewer. This time it is Tristan who turns Victoria down in a reversal of their roles from earlier in the film. Humphrey, Victoria's fiancé, appears just in time to witness this scene and promptly draws his short sword to challenge Tristan, but Tristan's leitmotif returns on French horn as he too draws his sword (with a Captain Shakespeare-esque flourish), and Humphrey quickly backs down. The leitmotif plays a key role in relating the scene to Tristan's earlier encounters with Victoria and Humphrey, reinforcing the many visual parallels but also suggesting how Tristan has changed in the interceding period, especially in comparison to the others. The use of cor Anglais followed by French horn for his melody echoes the earlier cue (1M6A), but the familiar timbres help make connections to the young Tristan without returning him to that character state. The rhythmic expansion of his theme is important in this regard, since it is a clear development of the original, hasty melody. Additionally, in this late cue the French horn plays the first rather than the second part of Tristan's melody; the "Tristan's Failure" leitmotif is neither implied nor heard on his return to Wall.

Figure 5.4. Tristan's leitmotif as it appears in 6M61. The rhythmic value of each note is doubled for a sense of gravitas and maturity, reflecting the development of his character

Tristan and The Royal Family of Stormhold

The "Royal Family" leitmotif is a minor-key version of the "Tristan" leitmotif, and forms the basis of a theme that is associated with ascension to the throne of Stormhold. The similarity of the leitmotifs provides a link between Tristan and the royal family, but the change of tonality masks the relationship to an extent and indicates that the characters themselves are unaware of the connection. The first member of the royal family to be associated with its leitmotif is Secundus, when he makes his grand entrance to the King of Stormhold's chamber (2M11 Alt).[6] The "Secundus" variation of the theme retains the two note anacrusis, but the following rhythmic values are extended affording the music greater weight than its parent material (Eshkeri uses this technique similarly in 6M61, as discussed above). The scoring—four French horns in unison—emphasizes the importance and regality of the person being presented, while also recalling the second phrase of Tristan's own melody through the shared timbre.

Figure 5.5. "Secundus"

Secundus's potential importance is enhanced by another cue devoted to him later in the same scene, though in the event this second cue underscores his death at the hands of Septimus. Eshkeri's original cue (2M12) uses a modified form of the "Royal Family" leitmotif as the basis for the melodic content, reversing the order of the opening four-notes and dropping the dominant down an octave so that the melody starts with an uncharacteristic rising minor 6th (see Figure 5.6). Overlapping layers of melody all utilize this structure before descending runs match Secundus's fall from the window and a brief timpani solo recalls the principal motif of Mahler's Fifth Symphony and its connotations of fate. 2M12 was written and recorded in mid April 2007, but it seems that a decision was taken quite late that an alternative cue was required, 2M12 Alt being composed in mid May and recorded at the final sessions on 25 May 2007. This second cue uses the "Secundus" melody for the material that precedes the descending runs and timpani solo, but in the event it is the original cue that appears in the film. Accordingly, Secundus's minute in the limelight is bookended by the "Royal Family" leitmotif: he is introduced by it, and his death is heralded by it heard in reverse.

Figure 5.6. The "Royal Family" leitmotif modified and used backwards multiple times in 2M12 "Secundus Dies"

Tristan's future as King of Stormhold is indicated by the use of the "Royal Family" leitmotif as the dying monarch enchants the ruby that will determine the next ruler (2M14A Part 1). The French horn timbre serves to link 2M14A Part 1 with Tristan's melody, but the minor key again obscures some of the connections (see Figure 5.7). The cue quickly moves onto other material (more on which below), but the opening serves as a further indication of Tristan's destiny and demonstrates the narrative agency of the score.

Figure 5.7. Opening melody of 2M14A Part 1, showing a rhythmically augmented version of the "Royal Family" leitmotif

There are two further uses of the "Royal Family" leitmotif prior to Tristan's coronation. The first occurs as the living princes of Stormhold, Primus, Tertius and Septimus, share a toast with the bishop in his chambers ahead of embarking on their individual quests for the ruby (3M20R), an act that results in the poisoning of the bishop, Tertius and apparently Septimus as well (see Figure 5.8). Thinking himself the final surviving heir, Primus lifts the crown from the altar in front of him to the sound of the "Royal Family" leitmotif, though his joy and the music are both cut short by Septimus laughing. It was he who planted the poison hoping to kill his two brothers, the music reflecting his sarcastic laughter and applause at Primus's expense. The accompaniment drops out of the texture part by part, almost in embarrassment, and there is a crude descending glissando on the final melody note, a pre-planned effect that was implemented at the recording session (see Figure 4.7), though it is not marked in the score.

Figure 5.8. End of 3M20R, as Primus believes himself the last surviving heir of Stormhold

The other occurrence follows Septimus's discovery of Primus's dead body at the site of Lamia's inn (4M37R), the leitmotif accompanying Septimus's declaration that he is king since his last brother is now dead. However, just as he intruded on Primus's moment of apparent glory in the bishop's chamber, so his brother (now a ghost) stops him in his tracks. Although the ghosts are never seen or heard by the other characters, their presence and words often influence the thoughts and actions of the living characters. As a result, when Primus observes that his brother is "not yet" king since he has not recovered the ruby, the thought also occurs to Septimus, bringing an abrupt end to the melody. Eshkeri has circled the final note of the horn melody and written "comedy fall?" in red pencil, but whereas this effect was utilized in 3M20R, no such comic feature is present in 4M37R.

Sandwiched between Primus's and Septimus's short-lived moments of triumph are two further cues that draw on Tristan's leitmotif to show character development and further connections between the protagonist and the monarchy of Stormhold. Following a dream in which he is informed of the danger that awaits Yvaine at Lamia's hands, Tristan's leitmotif gives rise to a melodic variation that attests to his new status as Yvaine's would-be savior rather than her captor (3M31). The theme (Figure 5.9) is proclaimed by unison French horns and trumpets imbuing it with a heroic impetus, but contrasts markedly with the material used to accompany the princes; the use of the leitmotif in its original major form at the outset maintains the connection to Tristan.

Figure 5.9. Heroic variation of Tristan's leitmotif

The melody is inflected into minor tonal areas after the initial fanfare statement, linking it more closely to the "Royal Family" leitmotif but also subtly hinting at the failure of Tristan's immediate quest—to catch the coach that is passing through the forest. His brave leap towards the vehicle leads only to him bouncing off it, though he does succeed in stopping it through his actions. The driver, Primus, is suspicious of him, assuming him to be an (inept) assassin sent by Septimus and approaches the prone Tristan with menace. This action is accompanied by a short figure that draws on the "Royal Family" leitmotif and is the only material in the score explicitly connected with Primus (the cue, 3M31A, is called "Primus"). The figure is little more than the leitmotif itself, which returns to the tonic and then drops a further semitone to an unresolved dissonance (see Figure 5.10). Although it is associated only with Primus this is the only use of the motif in the entire score since he dies in the following scene.

Figure 5.10. "Primus"

Tristan and Yvaine

The developing relationship between Tristan and Yvaine is reinforced by narrative connections in the musical score. 5M49 "Hedge Love" and 5M55 Alt "Mouse Love" both include connections to Tristan through the use of his leitmotif and the timbre of the cor Anglais. The former cue is based on Eshkeri's love theme, a musical idea never heard in full in the film but that displays strong links to Tristan's leitmotif through the prominence of the major arpeggio in the construction of the melody. The opening four notes outline the "Tristan" leitmotif, and the two-phrase structure of the theme recalls the similar bipartite nature of Tristan's own melody (see Figure 5.11). Yvaine, whose individual musical identity is considered in detail below, is represented in this cue by the flute. The cor Anglais acts as Tristan's voice, drawing on the connection between the character and the timbre established early in the film rather than demonstrating any regression of his personality or stature. This combination of instruments is revisited at the close of 5M55 Alt, the cor Anglais presenting material based on Tristan's leitmotif in that cue.

Figure 5.11. Opening flute melody of 5M49 "Hedge Love"

Tristan and His Destiny

The fight scene at the witches' lair includes two brief references to the "Royal Family" leitmotif. Each time the music is associated with Tristan (all the princes are dead), though it plays only a small part in the cue that houses it. There is a short horn figure, just the first three notes of the leitmotif, heard as Tristan faces the Mormo (7M70), the apparent futility of his effort reflected in his music being subordinate in the cue. After successfully disposing of the witch, the leitmotif is heard in full at the start of the following cue as he prepares to face Lamia herself (7M71), though their relative power is similarly reflected in the musical balance of the cue. The leitmotif is never associated with his own bravery or achievement in combat simply because it is not he who scores the final victory; Lamia is defeated by Yvaine (albeit enabled by Tristan), meaning that the final use of the leitmotif comes not in battle, but in celebration.

It is in the concluding coronation scene that both visual and musical narratives finally confirm that Tristan is a member of the royal family, and having recovered the ruby in the aftermath of the fight with the witches he is duly crowned King of Stormhold (7M76/77). The "Royal Family" leitmotif is heard on French horn as the ruby regains its color in Tristan's hand, and the music that follows to underscore the change of scene into the coronation uses the underlying chord progression of the heroic melody based on Tristan's leitmotif. Eshkeri holds the melody back until Tristan and Yvaine are crowned, at which point the "Royal Family" leitmotif finally reaches its full potential in a full orchestral version. It is followed by new melodic material that soars over the harmonic structure of this coronation theme and links into a grandiose version of the Love Theme, led by horns and trumpets. This last instance of the love theme and, accordingly, of Tristan's leitmotif indicates the end of his story (notwithstanding the film's epilogue) and his development from child to adult, ignorant to enlightened, shop-boy to king. It reconciles Tristan and Yvaine with his family heritage through the use of minor (royal) and major (love) versions of Tristan's leitmotif within the same cue, finally bringing into full view (and audibility) the connections between these musical branches of the score. It also allows the majestic implications evident in the music since the French horn solo in the second half of 1M6A to come to the fore as Tristan meets his destiny. Additionally, the final iteration of the leitmotif is in G major, the same key as the first, a final confirmation that Tristan will never again return to Wall, and that he has made Stormhold his home.

Captain Shakespeare and the Pirates

As discussed in Chapter 2, Eshkeri initially intended to use the motif from the opening of the score to represent Captain Shakespeare. The motif is striking, consisting of an ascending tonic-dominant-tonic melodic line followed by a dissonant sharp fourth that resolves onto the major third, and has overtones of the opening of Richard Strauss's tone poem, *Also Sprach Zarathustra*, famously used as the theme for *2001: A Space Odyssey* (1968). The major tonality implied by the final note of the motif is countered somewhat by the raised fourth, which gives rise to alternatives including the Lydian mode, acoustic scale, and octatonic scale. The raised 4th could simply be read as a chromatic inflection within the theme, though such an analysis would also allow it to be interpreted as whole tone (the E♮ simply being a flattened F♯), which seems less likely considering the sound of the phrase. The various harmonic options are shown in Figure 5.12, below; scale degrees that do not appear in the motif are reduced in size for clarity, and boxes show pitches that conflict with those in the melody, or are missing from the stated scale.

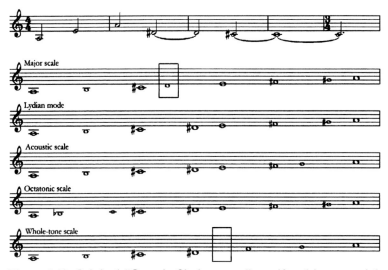

Figure 5.12. Original "Captain Shakespeare" motif and its potential harmonic implications

Analysis of the material that accompanies the motif at the start of the film shows that it features numerous D♯s and G♯s, supporting a reading of the music as based on the acoustic scale. As discussed in Chapter 4, Eshkeri initially brought the motif back into the score as the film title appears on the screen at the end of 1M4 "Snowdrop," again accompanied by shimmering, acoustic-scale based textures, but this ending was excised before the final cut of the film following conversations with Vaughn, who felt that it should not be used again in the score after its initial statement.[7]

As was shown in Chapter 4, the music for the opening sequence was written early in the scoring process, and accordingly Eshkeri did not ever compose any music for the Captain that made use of this motif. However, when Shakespeare is introduced in 4M35 he is accompanied by a motif (Figure 5.13) that shares some features with the composer's intended figure. Although there is no opening arpeggio in the "Shakespeare" leitmotif, there is a prominent sharp fourth that in this case resolves downwards onto the minor rather than the major third. This change alters the whole character of the phrase, the leitmotif indicating danger and trepidation rather than lightness and excitement. The underlying harmony of the leitmotif is switched from the acoustic scale to the octatonic scale (starting with a tone rather than a semitone), a naturally darker pitch set, notwithstanding the triplet quaver A that functions like an acciaccatura at the start of the second phrase.

Figure 5.13. The "Shakespeare" leitmotif, based on the opening motif of the score

Eshkeri's leitmotif generates an air of uncertainty about the Captain's character through the prominent augmented second interval between the G♯ and F♮ and the use of dark timbres including muted horns, high bassoon, and low harp and strings. The music functions as an aural projection of the Captain designed to impose itself on the audience just as Shakespeare's physical presence intimidates Tristan and Yvaine. The "Shakespeare" leitmotif is absent as he questions his captives in the ship's hold, the soundtrack instead emphasizing the theatrical nature of the scene as the Captain pauses in his interrogation to allow the crew (who are listening at the door) to respond. However, his demeanor changes on Tristan's mention of the village of Wall, the music building to a dissonant climax as the Captain throws a body—ostensibly Tristan, but actually a manikin—over the side of the ship. The Captain's leitmotif is then heard in the horns and low strings as he drags a screaming Yvaine on deck, and again in a slight variation as he tells the crew he's taking her to his cabin and he is not to be disturbed on pain of death.

Shakespeare's barbaric actions are all the more believable for the casting of Robert De Niro in the role, and the menace in his leitmotif closely matches the Captain's personality as it is shown on screen. However, once safely within his quarters Shakespeare's persona changes completely, and the "Shakespeare" leitmotif abruptly disappears from the score with the revelation of his true nature. It is replaced by two related melodies that represent the whole of the pirate crew, and that bear some relation to the "Tristan" leitmotif through their opening three pitches, albeit in a minor key like the material for the royal family. The same pitch set can also be identified at the start of the "Shakespeare" leitmotif, once the dissonant sharp 4th is removed, meaning that the two themes used to accompany the pirates can be seen as deriving from their Captain once he has lost his 'mean streak.'

The first of these new melodies (Figure 5.14b) is heard at points where the sky ship Caspartine comes in to land, firstly at the offices of Ferdy the Fence (5M43) and secondly to allow Tristan and Yvaine to disembark and head for Wall (5M46); accordingly it is referred to here as the "Boat" theme. Although occurring second in the film, the other melody (Figure 5.14a) was actually written first, since it is part of the pirate montage sequence (5M45A) that Eshkeri wrote as a demo for Paramount in July 2006. This theme is more associated with life aboard the ship, and is considered here as the "Pirate" theme as a result. The opening of the

"Boat" theme can be seen in the running line of the "Pirate" theme, and the hemiolas that follow draw on the rhythmic idea first presented in 3M31 with Tristan's heroic attempt to leap onto Primus's passing coach.

Figure 5.14a. "Pirate" theme as heard in 5M45A "Pirate Montage"

Figure 5.14b. "Boat" theme as heard in 5M46 "Boat Landing"

Yvaine

Rather than having her own distinctive theme, Yvaine is represented musically by a small set of elements depending on the context in which she is seen or discussed. She is often defined in opposition to others, effectively presenting her as contrasting with or complementary to characters including Tristan and Lamia. Eshkeri's approach is unusual in such a thematic score, particularly bearing in mind Yvaine's centrality to all branches of the story, but it is perhaps her integrity to the various aspects of the plot that renders her ideal for this sort of musical treatment.[8]

Yvaine and Tristan

The nearest Eshkeri comes to allocating Yvaine a specific musical idea is in cues based on the love theme. As discussed above, Yvaine is represented by the flute in these cues, in dialogue with Tristan's cor Anglais, but the melodic material is at best shared between the two lovers. Its connections to Tristan's leitmotif favor him in any derivation of ownership, despite the gradual equalizing of their relationship as the film progresses, though the shared use of a chord progression (Tristan in 3M31, Yvaine in 7M74, and both in 7M76/77) provides an underlying musical connection between them that offers both parties an equal claim to its ownership.

Yvaine and the Stars

Although other stars play a limited role in *Stardust* (restricted to the telling of and inclusion within Tristan's dream), musical representations of Yvaine often focus on her as a star rather than an individual. The use of a wordless female choir indicates both the romantic and heavenly or ethereal nature of the stars, particularly since this timbre is often accompanied by strings and harp. The female voices also emphasize Yvaine's own femininity, reinforcing her connection with the natural world as outlined by Curry (see above). The only musical motif that is related to Yvaine is *Twinkle, Twinkle Little Star*, though again this relates more to her being a star than to her as an individual character.

As discussed in Chapter 3, the melody is strewn throughout the film, accompanying instances when stars are mentioned, some of Yvaine's words and actions, and in scenes where Yvaine or stars in general have some influence or are worthy of consideration. This last such application of *Twinkle* assists in the understanding of Tristan's mindset on his return to Wall (6M61), a cue discussed above for its use of Tristan's theme. Immediately following the initial statement of the "Tristan" leitmotif the first violins present a phrase of *Twinkle* complete except for its final tonic note. The melody gives Yvaine a presence within the scene despite her being absent from the physical location, and also indicates her continuing significance in Tristan's life through the unfinished nature of the music. The simple harmony moves towards a perfect cadence in D major with successive chords of E^7 and A^7 ($\sharp II^7$–V^7), but the anticipated tonic chord does not appear at all in the rest of the cue—Tristan has travelled a great distance with Yvaine, but it is not yet time to signal the close of their relationship.

Yvaine and Lamia

Throughout the film numerous devices are used to represent Yvaine and Lamia as opposites. Yvaine is initially costumed in a shimmering, silver gown that contrasts sharply with Lamia's drab, black attire, and whereas the witch continues to age and become more decrepit as the film progresses, the star retains her youth and beauty.[9] Similarly, as Yvaine's attitude towards Tristan changes she becomes more amenable (both to him and the audience), whereas Lamia's increasing desperation to capture the star is reflected in the disintegration of her character through the film. The climax of the narrative places these personality transformations into stark contrast; Lamia's rejoicing at her sisters' deaths is the ultimate peak of her selfishness, whereas it is the love Yvaine has developed for Tristan that enables her to shine and kill the witch.

Eshkeri's score similarly sets Yvaine and Lamia in opposition, though since both are magical creatures they also share some musical characteristics. Chord progressions feature in the identities of both, with Yvaine's generally harmonically simple and tonal, and Lamia's intensely chromatic, moving outside normal tonal bounds. Yvaine's first such progression is heard as she falls from the sky as a star (2M14B), before she is seen as a woman. Sweeping descending string lines and a wordless female choir are the prominent timbres in a full orchestral texture, and the harmonic progression (Am–F–C–G–Am) uses shared pitches to move smoothly between the various chords. The first instance of the witches' chord progression occurs in the following cue (2M15), following Lamia's observation of the falling star. The short progression, Cm–C♯m–Cm, includes no shared pitches in consecutive chords, and the central C♯m chord jars against the underlying Cm harmony as a result. This first instance of the progression is atypical since the music also integrates aspects of the 'magic' texture (discussed in Chapter 3), and the witch chords are usually presented using low, dark timbres, with no movement or decoration in the texture. Female voices are used within Lamia's music, though to a far lesser extent than for Yvaine. The choir links Lamia's mission to Yvaine, and its employ also draws on the traditions of horror scoring.

Yvaine and Lady Una

Although they do not meet properly until the closing scenes of the film, Yvaine and Lady Una are connected through their shared representation by the flute, in addition to more intrinsically musical features as outlined below.

Lady Una

Lady Una has her own distinct musical leitmotif (Figure 5.15), first heard when Tristan's father, Dunstan, meets her at the market stall in the opening prologue. She is not introduced at this point—although she tells Dunstan she is a captive princess, the royal family has not yet appeared and her identity and name are only revealed in the closing scenes—and it is initially unclear whether the leitmotif represents her or the glass snowdrop she gives to Dunstan. The cue, 1M4, is called "Snowdrop" in all of the surviving documentation, and it is Una's utterance of this word that triggers the music in the film. It is only with the reappearance of the theme as Tristan and his father discuss her that the association can finally be made between music and character.

Figure 5.15. "Una"

Una's theme can be seen to bear traces of the "Royal Family" leitmotif, though it is not as pronounced as in the music that accompanies the males. The first three pitches of the minor scale, the opening of that leitmotif, feature significantly, though they do not appear in ascending order as is the case in the princes' material. Instead, the short descending scales in the "Lady Una" leitmotif serve to associate her with the monarchy, but to keep this connection hidden, reflecting her circumstances.

Una's music also connects her to Yvaine, and in addition to the flute timbre (chosen for Una owing to its connection to birdsong),[10] these characters are linked by the use of the flattened 6th degree of the scale in their principal musical motifs. The start of the "Lady Una" leitmotif can even be seen as the opening of *Twinkle, Twinkle Little Star* without the initial note. The flattened sixth (A♭ in Example 5.15, above) emphasizes the exotic 'otherness' of both women, a characteristic that is arguably shared with Lamia, the top line of whose chords also match the opening of Una's theme (the Cm–C♯m–Cm progression outlined above yields a top line of G–G♯/A♭–G). Whereas the story's principal men—Tristan, Septimus, Primus and Shakespeare—are essentially human in all that they do, the leading women—Yvaine, Lamia and Una—are mysterious and magical characters, reflecting the whole world of Stormhold.[11]

Stormhold

Though it is not really a character, and not strictly 'good,' Stormhold is represented musically in a manner that links it to the characters and themes already discussed.[12] There is one principal "Stormhold" melody (Figure 5.16), first heard in the opening prologue when the idea of another world existing beyond the wall is mooted. As discussed in Chapter 4, the first occurrence of the "Stormhold" theme omits the melody, presenting just the harmonic outline for the theme under the voiceover, meaning that when the cor Anglais enters with the melodic material six bars later it is actually a variation of theme that has not yet been heard.

Figure 5.16. "Stormhold"

The "Stormhold" theme introduces several musical ideas that permeate the score. Melodically, the use of C♯ and C♮ in successive bars results in the theme alternating between major and minor tonal areas, mirroring the relationship between the "Tristan" and "Royal Family" leitmotifs. The underlying harmony alternates between bars of A major and F major, chords linked by a common pitch (A) that functions as a pivot, much like the progression that is often used to represent Yvaine/stars, and the use of a pedal tone with changing harmonies above it also features in the musical representation of Lamia and the witches. Although the witches' harmonies are usually dissonant where the Stormhold harmonies are consonant, it still serves to reinforce the link between the fantasy world and its inhabitants. The sharpened 4th that results from the F major harmony in the second bar of the theme (B♮) creates a link to the "Shakespeare" leitmotif and also ties the material to the very opening of the film. The latter connection characterizes Stormhold as a place of magic, though the dissonance is not so prominent as to draw attention to it, in keeping with Vaughn's intention that magic should be treated as an everyday occurrence on the fantasy side of the wall.

The "Stormhold" melody can also be analyzed as consisting of the first three notes of a major scale followed by the same degrees of a minor scale, reaffirming its connection with Tristan, the royal family, and the pirates, and it is often used in conjunction with Tristan and Yvaine, linking these two 'outsiders' with Stormhold and hinting at their future integration into the very fabric of that world. A variation on the theme (Figure 5.17) accompanies the flashback of Una writing her letter to Tristan and placing it in his Moses basket (2M18). Although the reading of the letter occurs in Wall (in Dunstan's attic), the flashback takes place in Sal's caravan in Stormhold, and the music positions the visual action on that side of the wall. The variation draws on the major/minor characteristics of the theme, combining a G major ascending and a G minor descending line over G minor and E♭ major harmonies respectively.

Figure 5.17. Variation on "Stormhold" from 2M18 "Una's Letter," combining major and minor melodic phrases with opposing harmonies

'Evil' Characters

Paulus observes that there are not as many 'evil' characters as 'good' in *Star Wars*, and accordingly there are fewer 'evil' themes in the score, though they maintain a strong presence across the films.[13] The same principle is true of *Stardust*, in which Lamia (and by extension her sisters) is the main antagonist. Madame Semele/Ditchwater Sal also comes into this category and, although he has been considered above as part of the royal family of Stormhold, Septimus also appears in the following discussion since his actions are always motivated by personal gain rather than by any wish to assist Tristan. Additionally, it can be argued that Septimus is as evil as Lamia by the closing scenes, since he seeks Yvaine for her heart in addition to the power of Stormhold, with the selfish aim of ruling the kingdom forever.

Lamia and the Witches

Numbers play a key role in the construction of *Stardust*. Each of the princes of Stormhold is surrounded by his birth number in ways ranging from the size of their riding party (Primus is alone on the coach, Septimus is always accompanied by six other riders to take his total to seven), to the Roman numerals embroidered onto their outfits, and Eshkeri transfers that principle to his representation of the witches. The music for Lamia, Mormo and Empusa is based on the number three, most clearly identified in the use of three triadic chords as their main leitmotif. First heard in 2M15, as outlined above, the progression initially features three chords, the outer two of which are the same with the central harmony set at a higher pitch. Initially this is a minor 3rd, the first instance of the "Witch Chords" leitmotif sounding as Cm–E♭m–Cm, though it quickly reduces to a semitone (Cm–C♯m–Cm), and intervals of a semitone and a tritone (a further derivative of three) are the most commonly used through the film. A variation of this pattern is used when Lamia is alone, a three-note oscillating line in which the middle pitch is a semitone higher than the outer notes usually placed in the bass or higher in the texture over a sustained bass note. The reduction from chords to single pitches indicates the presence of one witch rather than all three.

Figure 5.18. Reduction of bars 17–25 of 2M15 "Lamia's Youth," showing the "Witch Bassline" leitmotif and the "Witch Chords" leitmotif deriving from it

The witches are also associated with an angular, dissonant bass line, first heard at the very start of 2M15 (Figure 5.18), and which actually gives rise to the "Witch Chords" progression. This figure is based around the quaver repetition of a single pitch, the line punctuated by short silences and dissonant semitones and tritones. Although not initially based on the idea of 'three,' the "Witch Bassline" leitmotif is a crucial component in the musical construction of Lamia and her sisters, and develops significantly as the film progresses.

One or both of the witch leitmotifs appear in the majority of cues that focus on Lamia's branch of the narrative. Three triadic three-chord phrases are heard as she prepares to leave the witches' lair on her quest to kill the star (3M21), Eshkeri varying the leitmotif's central interval from semitone to tritone and finally minor 3rd, again mimicking the structure of the witches' bassline. The time signature then shifts to ¾ and a triple-time derivative of the "Witch Bassline" leitmotif is introduced in the cellos (Figure 5.19), soon joined by low woodwinds, timpani and double basses, injecting the scene with urgency as Lamia departs. The bassline is present as the witches kill the crocodile to determine the star's location (3M28), and the "Witch Chords" leitmotif is heard as Lamia and her sisters discuss her failed trap (4M38) and Yvaine's proximity to the dividing wall (6M59R). As the film approaches its climax, both leitmotifs feature as Lamia kills Sal and abducts Yvaine and Lady Una (6M63), the cue finishing with the triple-time variation on the "Witch Bassline" ominously hammered out on timpani played with hard sticks. However, the two sequences that feature the witches most prominently vary considerably in the employment and development of their musical material.

Figure 5.19. Triple-time derivative of the "Witch Bassline" leitmotif

Lamia's Inn (4M32, 4M33 and 4M34)

The music that accompanies the extended scene at Lamia's inn is spread across three cues labeled as parts 1 to 3. Although there are natural break points in the dramatic action at the transitions between cues (the arrival of Primus and Tristan at the inn, and Lamia's murder of Primus), as discussed in Chapter 4 most of the sustained musical passages in *Stardust* were broken down into several parts by Steve McLaughlin in order to expedite the approval process. The musical underscoring for the scene at the inn lasts for nearly eight minutes, and gaining Vaughn's approval for a single cue spanning the whole duration would have been much more difficult than obtaining it for three shorter cues. A problem with a short section of a long cue would have resulted in the entire cue being rejected, meaning that no part of it could have been passed on to the orchestrator; by breaking the music up into three parts, a similar issue with a small section of the underscore would have resulted in the two unaffected cues progressing through the score-production process while the problematic cue was revised. Indeed, the lack of a gap between 4M33 and 4M34 indicates strongly that the division of the material into three parts was done for the convenience of the creative team rather than for dramatic reasons.

The sequence opens with the "Witch Chords" leitmotif as Yvaine rides the unicorn towards the inn, but once she enters the building there is no trace of the witches in the music. Just as Lamia hides her true identity and motivations from her prey, so too the music refuses to acknowledge her presence. Instead, Eshkeri draws on J.S. Bach's Prelude no. 2 in C minor BWV847 from book 1 of *Das Wohltemperierte Klavier* to provide the bulk of the musical and particularly the harmonic framework for the scene. The prelude was chosen by Eshkeri firstly because of his love of Bach's music, but also because it carries a sense of inevitability through the harmonic progression, and this is beneficial for increasing the tension as the scene progresses. In an email to orchestrator Nick Ingman, Eshkeri said that the cue is "inspired by, and in many ways is a variation on, a famous piece of classical music,"[14] and he has remarked that he inserted little quotes such as this "because it's a fun score" (*Stardust* being the fairy tale that won't behave), and "it's interesting for the players too."[15]

The choice of Bach may prompt comparisons with other scores that use 'high art' music to accompany 'evil' characters,[16] though it is clear that Eshkeri's purpose in this instance was to provide a structure within which he could weave thematic elements without obstructing the inexorable progression of the music. Bach's harmony runs uninterrupted from bar 12 to bar 30 of the cue—the entire first half of the Prelude—and Eshkeri seamlessly interpolates a bass melody for low winds and strings, a solo for contrabassoon, a variation on the "Stormhold" leitmotif played on flute, and elements that reflect Lamia's use of magic to heal Yvaine's injured leg. When Bach is finally left behind the cue continues in a similar vein, the harmonic progression showing no signs of deviation from its original course, and a moving quaver line shared by harp and celesta masking the change from old master to young composer. *Twinkle, Twinkle Little Star* makes an appearance as Yvaine starts to glow, but even as Lamia reaches for her knife the witch material remains steadfastly absent.

As if to compensate, the remaining two parts of the scene are dominated by a variation of the "Witch Bassline" leitmotif, though Eshkeri removes the chromatic inflections to signify Lamia's loss of control and the revealing of her true identity as the scene progresses. Vaughn was keen that the music should incorporate a dance-like feel, and he and Eshkeri discussed the possible use of a Bolero rhythm in this section. These deliberations led to a development of the underlying quaver rhythm, which is enhanced to incorporate two sets of three notes; each bar contains triplet semiquavers followed by three quavers. However, while this rhythmic pattern fills the leitmotif with references to the number three, it also quotes an external source. In this case the piece is "Vampire Hunters" from Wojciech Kilar's score to Francis Ford Coppola's *Bram Stoker's Dracula* (1992), which also provides a stylistic model for Eshkeri's cue with its undulating bass melodies and dissonant chordal interjections (see Figure 5.20).

Figure 5.20. Basslines and bass melodies from Kilar's "Vampire Hunters" (top) and Eshkeri's 4M33 "Lamia's Inn Part 2" (bottom)[17]

There are undoubtedly similarities between the two cues, though arguably both can be seen as deriving from John Williams's "Imperial March" from *The Empire Strikes Back,* and beyond that to "Mars, Bringer of War" from Gustav Holst's suite *The Planets.* Those connections notwithstanding, Eshkeri's material is also clearly derived from musical ideas already present in his score. As outlined above, the rhythmic figure is a variation of the "Witch Bassline," and analysis of the melody shows that it is based on the "Royal Family" leitmotif, being structured around the first three pitches of the minor scale followed by a move to the dominant note. Indeed, although the scene is ostensibly about Lamia and Yvaine, this central section revolves around Primus who inadvertently interrupts Lamia's planned execution by his untimely arrival at the inn. That the melodic component of the cue should feature the musical hallmark of the royal family is therefore unsurprising, since the music runs from Primus's intrusion until his death when Lamia slits his throat. Extensions of the melody continue from the end of the leitmotif, hovering around the dominant note, the line shifting up and down in semitones in a subtle hint at the influence that Lamia will have on the prince. The music builds as Primus realizes that Yvaine has the Stormhold ruby, but even as the melody moves to the French horns with their regal implications, so too the rhythmic figure builds in instrumentation and dynamic until it overcomes the "Royal family" leitmotif as Primus dies.

There is no respite for Yvaine or Tristan, however, the music continuing into 4M34 without a break and, now, without the influence of the royal family. The pulsing rhythm returns but the melodic content of the cue now also derives from the witches' music, being comprised almost exclusively of semitone swells. Eshkeri also uses extended techniques to enhance the sense of the supernatural apparent in the visual images. Throughout 4M33 the music rose a perfect 5th at the end of each iteration of the melody, reaching A minor by the start of 4M34. This pattern continues throughout the third part of the scene moving onwards through E minor, but on reaching B minor there is change in the melody. As outlined in the discussion of Eshkeri's musical style in Chapter 2, the passage from bar 23 of "Lamia's Inn Part 3" foregrounds five-note ascending minor scales, the underlying harmony shifting down by first a major 3rd and then by minor 3^{rds} on completion of each sequence to enable the melodic line to continue its ascent. The irregularity of the harmonic rhythm—five bars is an unusual phrase length—coupled with the seemingly ever increasing pitch of the melody builds the tension for the climax of the scene as Lamia advances on her cornered prey, but her plot fails and Tristan and Yvaine escape using the last of the Babylon candle. Lamia's defeat is accompanied by a brief silence—the music seems as incredulous as she is that the star has slipped from her grasp—and the brief coda to the cue does not return to her music. Such is the disappointment of this episode that the witch material remains largely absent from the score until the final sequence, discussed below.

The Witches Lair (6M64 to 7M74)

Lamia's kidnapping of Yvaine and Lady Una sets Vaughn and Goldman's restructured 'third act' of *Stardust* in motion, and also heralds a prominent return of the witches' musical material. This section includes twelve cues, the majority of which feature variants on or derivations of the witch leitmotifs. The first cue in this section, 6M64 "Lamia Rides," reintroduces the triple-time variant of the "Witch Bassline" heard earlier as Lamia prepared to depart on her mission. The rhythmic drive of the music is retained as the action cross-cuts between Lamia's coach, Tristan, and Septimus (the latter two both on horseback) as they each make their way towards Lamia's lair. The only respite in the sequence comes when the music lapses into the "Witch Chords" leitmotif to underscore dialogue as Lamia is greeted by her sisters. Tristan is confronted outside the lair by Septimus, but their proximity to the witches results in most of the music that accompanies their exchange being drawn from the "Witch Chords" leitmotif (6M67). The leitmotifs are also featured as Septimus and Tristan face off with Empusa and Mormo in their individual battles (7M68 and 7M70 respectively). In each case a development of the "Witch Bassline" is used to mark the witch's attack or advance—Empusa throwing fire at

Septimus; Mormo running to engage Tristan—and their opponents are largely unrepresented in the underscoring. Septimus is accompanied in his battle by music that draws stylistically (if not harmonically) on the "Augurs of Spring" from Stravinsky's ballet *The Rite of Spring*. The repeated quaver motion punctuated by syncopated accented chords returns when Tristan fights with Lamia (7M71). Lamia's magic fails owing to the protective power of the glass snowdrop, the music hanging on the second chord of a three-chord progression as she changes tack, and the Stravinsky-esque material returns as she instead focuses on other ways to attack Tristan.

The pulsing quavers lead directly into a run of cues that accompany the climax of the fight—Tristan's swordfight with the zombie Septimus (7M72), his escape on the chandelier cable (7M72A), a further swordfight with Lamia (7M72B) and Lamia's apparent release of her prisoners (7M72C). As was shown in Chapter 2, the music for the zombie fight is based on Eshkeri's own score for *Colosseum*, and there is no reference to any other *Stardust* music in that cue or the one that follows it. 7M72B is underpinned by the triple-time "Witch Bassline" leitmotif, overlaid with extended techniques in the strings and loud accented chords in the brass and percussion, but when Lamia chooses to release rather than kill Tristan and Yvaine (7M72C) the music is largely devoid of her material, reinforcing the visual impression that she no longer seeks to kill the star. However, the music, like Lamia herself, is false. Her cries change to laughter as she magically locks the doors, and Tristan and Yvaine are herded back towards her by flying glass to the sound of the two witch leitmotifs (7M73). Lamia advances, knife in hand (7M74) to a melody in violas and bass flute derived from the "Witch Chords" leitmotif (Figure 5.21), but her victory is short-lived as Yvaine's chords emerge in a blaze of orchestral and vocal glory that mirrors her incandescence on screen and Lamia is destroyed.

Figure 5.21. Final melody derived from the "Witch Chords" leitmotif

The witches' leitmotifs each spawn a number of melodic ideas as the narrative progresses, but they do not develop in the same way as Tristan's does. This may be because the most significant development would be required during the 'third act,' and this was the part of the film that was most often revised during post-production owing in part to the inclusion of so many special effects. The general score production timeline shows that the material for reel 7 of the film was among the last to be written—that it had the shortest available turnaround time between composition and final recording—which may explain why there is so much use of unrelated musical material in addition to the cue derived from *Colosseum*. Alternatively it can be considered that the leitmotifs do not develop significantly because they accurately mirror the witches, each of whom dies with the same intention they had at the start of the film, namely to kill the star and consume her heart. Their leitmotifs may not have developed in the way that Tristan's has, but, then again, neither have their characters.

Madame Semele/Ditchwater Sal

Sal is seen very briefly in the long opening scene, when the young Dunstan Thorn approaches her market stall, and her motif was originally to have been heard at this point. As outlined in Chapter 4, Vaughn felt the intricacy of Eshkeri's original cue (which also introduced the "Lady Una" leitmotif) unduly cluttered the scene, so the references to these two motifs were removed. Accordingly, Sal does not gain a musical representation until later in the story, when Lamia happens upon her at the roadside. A simple motif is heard in the bass that characterizes Sal's rustic and uncultured background (Figure 5.22a). The subtle inclusion of the single-note "Witch Chords" leitmotif, a semitone oscillation, indicates that she has magical abilities, but not on the same scale as Lamia and her sisters. As a minor character in the story (she is not as crucial to the film as she is to the novel), Sal's leitmotif does not feature particularly often and is not subject to very much development. However, Eshkeri does use a variant of the leitmotif to comic effect when, after she loses her duel with Lamia, Sal's headless body staggers around before bumping into the wall and falling to the floor (Figure 5.22b).

Figure 5.22a. "Sal"

Figure 5.22b. Variant of the "Sal" leitmotif used after she is killed by Lamia

Septimus

As discussed in Chapter 3, the original "Septimus" theme (Figure 5.23) was one of the two pieces written by Eshkeri as a demo for Paramount in July 2006, and although the melody appears in numerous places in the *Stardust* score, there is no specific cue with this name. The theme has a time signature of $\frac{7}{8}$, consistently phrased in a 2+2+3 pattern, as a musical reflection of Septimus's status as the seventh son.

Figure 5.23. The "Septimus" theme

As the name and numeric connection indicate, the cue was conceived as a leitmotif for Septimus, but as the project continued it became apparent that this musical material worked well in a dramatic sense beyond the confines of such a strict relationship. Accordingly, it is often used to accompany action scenes, those with chasing and horse-riding, the relentless quaver movement generating energy and tension amplified by the irregular beat pattern that sometimes includes single bars of $\frac{5}{8}$, $\frac{9}{8}$ and even $\frac{11}{8}$ (in each case the music is scored as a series of quaver pairs with an extended final beat). However, the theme can still be seen to have a tangential relationship to Septimus. Its use to accompany shots of Primus's coach implies Septimus's dominance over his brothers (who ride within the coach as Primus drives), the music hovering specter-like around their futile search for the Stormhold ruby and an aural signal that if any of the brothers is to succeed it will be the youngest of them. Septimus's apparent succession is implied from the earliest use of material in $\frac{7}{8}$, as the enchanted necklace shoots into the sky from the royal palace (2M14A Part 2). Although the "Septimus" theme is not heard in full until the pursuit begins, when it accompanies first Septimus and then Primus as they start their quests (3M24), the early association of the rhythmic figure with the chase for the ruby creates an implication that Septimus is the favorite to recover the stone.

The widespread use of the "Septimus" theme across the film for action and travelling scenes led to the creation of a new leitmotif for the character, though this only features fleetingly in the score. The five-note motif (Figure 5.24) is based around the first three notes of a minor scale, and can accordingly be related back to the start of the "Royal Family" leitmotif. However, the pitches are presented out of sequence, somewhat masking the origins of the motif as well as lending an air of menace to the figure. His leitmotif also provides an additional bridge between the "Royal

Family" leitmotif and that of Lady Una; when the underpinning harmonies are considered it is apparent that both are based around the dominant note, and Septimus's leitmotif can be seen as a variation of Una's in retrograde.

Figure 5.24. The "Septimus" leitmotif

The leitmotif was first scored by Eshkeri at the start of cue 4M37, where Septimus arrives at the site of Lamia's inn and discovers his dead brother's body. The cue opens with a timpani roll and low strings that establish G as the tonal centre, the leitmotif entering on bassoon and horns in the third bar. However, the revised version of the cue (4M37R) substitutes a simplified version of the motif that extends the opening crotchet and omits the quavers, resulting in the single-note "Witch Chord" leitmotif played by violas and cellos. Whereas the original cue highlights Septimus as surveyor of the scene, the revision instead recalls the perpetrator, Lamia, even though Septimus is the visual focus. 4M37R continues with the "Royal Family" leitmotif as Septimus declares himself king—this theme is absent from 4M37—but it subsides rapidly as he realizes he still needs the ruby to claim the throne. It is only here that his leitmotif finally appears in 4M37R, the original cue presenting a decorated version of the phrase at this point. The cue heard in the film is an amalgam of 4M37 and 4M37R, the latter of which is a much shorter cue in the notated score indicating strongly that the revision was only ever designed to replace the first part of the cue. Accordingly, the first fifteen bars are 4M37R, reverting to 4M37 for the remaining twenty-eight bars of the music.

With regard to Septimus, the most significant aspect of this revision is that his leitmotif is withheld until later in the cue, and the distinct similarities between his motif and the single-note "Witch Chord" leitmotif are laid bare in the opening bars. The musical connection Eshkeri makes between the prince and the witches is apt, since it is in this scene that Septimus becomes aware of Yvaine's existence and decides to hunt her in addition to the stone. The leitmotif returns on three further occasions, each of which shows Septimus in a different context. The first follows his escape from Shakespeare's pirate crew (5M52), the leitmotif appearing in ⅞ and in a slightly developed form that links it more closely to the "Septimus" theme, albeit that it is still based around the dominant rather than the tonic note. The modification of the theme does not relate particularly to any change in Septimus's character, but its presence perhaps indicates that he got more out of his encounter with Captain Shakespeare than is shown on screen; he is next seen riding on the road to the wall despite Shakespeare claiming not to have told him where Tristan and Yvaine were heading. The last two instances occur during the scene at the witches' lair at the climax of the film. The first iteration announces his arrival to the audience and Tristan (6M67), and the second is heard as he advances on Lamia and Mormo having disposed of Empusa (7M69). In each case the leitmotif is stated singly and simply in the manner of a musical signpost, with no consideration of character development or particular narrative agency. However, like the witches (or, in fact, all of the 'evil' characters), Septimus does not undergo significant character development as the story progresses, so it is understandable that this is reflected in his leitmotif.

Reading the Music of *Stardust*

As has been shown, the musical landscape of *Stardust* consists largely of a number of inter-connected themes that represent most of the principal and minor characters. This "web of leitmotifs," to use Paulus's terminology, lends the score coherence and offers deeper insights into the relationships between the various characters, in addition to helping define their roles as 'good' or 'evil' in the context of the narrative. As outlined in Chapter 4, Eshkeri's early "Ruff *Stardust* Idea v3" can be seen as the foundation upon which many of the principal leitmotifs are based, with others forming as developments of these basic themes as has been shown above. The other key source in this regard is *Twinkle, Twinkle Little Star*.

The various connections across *Stardust*'s web of leitmotifs are shown in Figure 5.25, below. The two source themes appear at the top of the web,[18] but while other melodies have been placed within the framework with due consideration to their role in the various hierarchical and developmental structures that exist in both the music and the filmic narrative, strict interpretation of position as a correlate to importance is not always possible on the grounds of practicality. The "Royal Family" leitmotif, for instance, can be seen as deriving directly from "Ruff *Stardust* Idea v3" as well as being a minor-key version of the "Tristan" leitmotif, and appears lower in the web than "Tristan's Failure" purely on the grounds of available space. The four extracts at the bottom of the figure do not relate directly to either of the key sources for the score, though loose connections can be argued for both "Stormhold" and the motif from the prologue, the latter of which is the source for "Shakespeare." The material in $\frac{7}{8}$ has been retitled as the "Action/Travelling" motif to avoid confusion with the "Septimus" leitmotif (Figures 5.23 and 5.24 respectively).

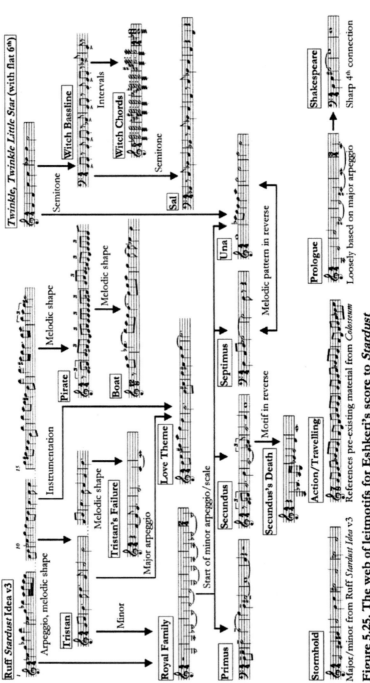

Figure 5.25. The web of leitmotifs for Eshkeri's score to *Stardust*

The importance of the arpeggio is apparent from the opening phrase of "Ruff *Stardust* Idea v3," and although the harmony of the passage is resolutely minor, taken in isolation the melody can be seen as outlining overlapping major and minor arpeggios (E♭–G–B♭, and G–B♭–D). The duality of these arpeggio figures reflects the relationship between the "Tristan" and "Royal Family" leitmotifs, and the oboe theme that enters with the pick-up to bar 10 is a clear pre-cursor to Tristan's cor Anglais melody, albeit in a minor key. The succeeding dialogue between the oboe and flute anticipates the timbres Eshkeri employs to represent Tristan and Yvaine, and also marks the influence of his training in the Kamen tradition. A clear source for the "Pirate" and "Boat" themes can be found in the passage from bar 15 (the third part of "Ruff *Stardust* Idea v3" shown in Figure 5.25), with two short phrases based around a descending pattern followed by a version of the theme proper. The final melodies as found in the score are an amalgam of the opening notes of the "Tristan" leitmotif (in the minor) and the melodic shape of bars 17–18, though both leitmotifs are underpinned by driving triple-time quavers, evoking the idea of a sea shanty that is understandably absent from the early sketch.

The centrality of the number three in the musical construction of Lamia and the witches has already been considered in detail, but it can also be seen to hold significant influence across the score in general. The 'good' leitmotifs are generally based around the interval of a third (major or minor), and most of these leitmotifs open with the first three notes of a scale. The love theme is perhaps the most extreme example of this significance—the melody begins with the first three notes of a D major scale, which is followed by a succession of minor and major thirds as the melody progresses (F♯–A–F♯–D–B)—and the main "Tristan" leitmotif can be seen as comprising the start of a scale with the addition of the interval of a minor 3rd to reach the dominant note, before the opening three pitches return.

The various relationships between the leitmotifs in *Stardust* have been explored in the above analysis and are crystallized in Figure 5.25. The interconnected nature of Eshkeri's themes results in the score doing far more than merely providing musical signposting, and several leitmotifs are used to reflect character and narrative development as the film progresses. While some aspects of the score serve to reinforce interpretations of the visual images—such as the grand entrance music of Secundus, which contributes to Vaughn's desire that viewers should consider the character important to the plot—other parts bring additional elements into the filmic narrative, supplementing what is seen on screen. The separation of Eshkeri's leitmotifs into 'good' and 'bad' groups, each with their own principal musical source, acts as an aural replacement for the idea of the

"Fellowship of the Castle," since the music forms an apparent though unspoken kinship between Tristan and several other characters. Similarly, Tristan's development from a boy to a man—the premise of the story as outlined in one of Sir Ian McKellen's voiceovers—is evident through the development of his motif. The derivation of both the "Royal Family" and "Love" leitmotifs from Tristan's theme reflects the broadening of his character, and emphasizes the role Eshkeri's score plays in the presentation of the narrative through the musical signification of the various characters and relationships.

Reading a Fantasy Score in the Post-*Lord of the Rings* Era

Is it unfair, or is it expected, to compare the score for a fantasy film to Howard Shore's *Lord of the Rings*? To me—and I am not alone here—this trilogy as a whole is a five-star score, so in a sense, such a comparison is really just a more specific way of giving a rating out of five stars.[19]

With the enormous success of the *Harry Potter* and *Lord of the Rings* films, we have seen endless fantasy productions popping up left and right. [. . . Eshkeri's] music here sounds almost EXACTLY what you expect it to sound like: twinkling romance, sweeping strings for everything remotely dramatic, "dum-dum-dum-dum" action for the more energetic scenes.[20]

The top quotation, from Matt Brennan's review of the *Stardust* official soundtrack album puts into sharp focus the difficulties faced by composers of scores for fantasy films in the post-*Lord of the Rings* era. The immense popular success of Peter Jackson's adaptation of Tolkien's story meant that Howard Shore's score for *The Fellowship of the Ring* had an impact on the popular consumption of film music not witnessed since John Williams's score for *Star Wars: A New Hope* in 1977. The relationship between *Star Wars* and *The Lord of the Rings* in areas such as genre, narrative structure, issues of adaptation, and instances of homage or borrowing is discussed at length in the literature, though the lasting impact of the music is often overlooked in these considerations.[21] Film franchises such as the *Harry Potter* and *Pirates of the Caribbean* series have also added to the expectations of audiences and film-makers regarding what music for a fantasy film 'should' sound like—the second quotation above, from Clark Douglas, almost spells out the requirements of such a score[22]—placing increased pressure on composers to create music that meets these expectations without becoming derivative. The following reading draws on the previous analysis of Eshkeri's score to contextualize the music for *Stardust* within the canon of fantasy films in the post-*Lord of the Rings* era, bearing in mind Eshkeri's status and experience in the industry and the role of his musical and filmic influences in the formulation and development of the score.

As shown in Figure 5.25, Eshkeri's score is rooted principally in the sketch material he created in January 2007. However, there are also overtones of other scores evident in the music for *Stardust*, a natural consequence of the requirements incumbent on the composer to ensure his music was accepted into the fantasy canon. Eshkeri's main "Tristan" theme has been compared to Howard Shore's "The Shire Theme: Pensive Setting" from *The Lord of the Rings* by some reviewers.[23] However, such a comparison is based purely on a small fragment of melody—both motifs open with the first three notes of the major scale followed by a jump to the dominant—at the expense of the majority of the musical material. The two melodies diverge significantly from that point, and the underlying rhythmic and harmonic profiles of the themes are also completely different (Figure 5.26). However, just as the choice of Sir Ian McKellen lends authority to the voiceovers in *Stardust*, so too the allusion to Shore's motif, whether intentional or not, enhances the effectiveness of Eshkeri's "Tristan" leitmotif. Any perceived relationship between the two themes in the mind of a viewer lends weight to the establishment of Tristan's character as passive, quiet and unadventurous, traits that can also be associated with hobbits.

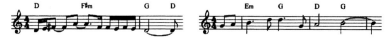

Figure 5.26. Opening of Shore's "The Shire Theme: Pensive Setting" (left) and Eshkeri's "Tristan" theme (right), showing the similarities in the initial melodic shape and differences in the rhythmic and harmonic profiles

In his analysis of Shore's music for *The Lord of the Rings*, Doug Adams observes that the score (considered as a composite across the three films) is based around the opening three notes of the "Shire" theme. Since Eshkeri's *Stardust* music derives largely from the "Tristan" leitmotif, itself based on a simple major scale and arpeggio, it is therefore unsurprising that some melodic similarities may exist between the scores. An apparent relationship between Eshkeri's "Boat" leitmotif and Shore's "Fellowship Theme" demonstrates this point, while simultaneously emphasizing the fact that consideration of a melodic fragment alone does not enable a proper analysis of the music, or understanding of its narrative role and connotations. Shore's melody is constructed of a three-pitch fanfare figure followed by a melodic phrase, a second fanfare, and a shorter concluding phrase. The theme is placed over exclusively major harmonies that often take the music away from the tonic key of D major, and is rhythmically predictable, with the main ♩ ♫ pattern featuring in six of its eight bars. Eshkeri's material differs significantly from Shore's in terms of both harmonic and rhythmic content, remaining much more predictably tonal and containing greater rhythmic variety and drive. The two themes are shown in Figure 5.27, below, to provide a comparison of their melodic, harmonic and rhythmic elements.

Figure 5.27. "Fellowship theme" from Howard Shore's score to *The Lord of the Rings* (top) and Eshkeri's "Landing" theme (bottom), showing the melodic, rhythmic and harmonic profiles of the two themes

With the removal of Shore's fanfares there are just two points at which the melodic profiles of these passages differ. Firstly, the plagal E♭–B♭ cadence in the third bar of Eshkeri's cue necessitates an E♭ in the melody where Shore's relentlessly major B♭–C–D progression includes an E♮. Shore's pitch is rather more prominent here owing to the chromatic nature of the harmony and the fact that each of the chords in his theme is allotted its own beat in a homorhythmic texture. Eshkeri's melody, by contrast, arises because of the inherent cadential progression, meaning that the D at the bottom of the phrase (where the cadence reaches the tonic chord of B♭) is the focal point of the line. The other melodic difference occurs towards the end of the passage, Eshkeri using the same melodic pattern twice in the penultimate bar where Shore varies the shape of his musical line. Again, however, there is a contrast in the focus of these melodies as Shore repeats the B♭–C–D progression that ended his first phrase, and Eshkeri complements the previous plagal cadence with an F^sus4–B♭ perfect cadence.

The connections between Eshkeri's "Boat" and "Pirate" leitmotifs have been made clear above, and both of these themes are derived from material in "Ruff *Stardust* Idea v3" that bears no obvious relationship to Shore's music. While a melodic similarity to Shore's "Fellowship" is apparent in the final cue, the harmonic and rhythmic profiles differ markedly creating contrasting emphases and impressions. Indeed just as the Kilar and Eshkeri cues outlined above (see Figure 5.20) can both be seen to have their roots in the music of Gustav Holst, so too can a common ancestor for these melodies be found in the Western classical canon. The second theme from the second movement of Rachmaninoff's Symphony no. 2 shares this melodic outline, but just as with the apparent connections between the Shore and Eshkeri themes, the link comes at the expense of harmonic progression and rhythmic profile. Accordingly, it is clear that neither composer has based their theme on Rachmaninoff's.

Figure 5.28. Second theme from the second movement of Rachmaninoff's Symphony no. 2 in E minor, Op. 27

The "Fellowship Theme" and "Boat" leitmotif are also treated differently in terms of timbre and texture, which sets them apart in the way they are interpreted and understood in their respective filmic contexts. Doug Adams describes Shore's theme as "receptive and sympathetic, but at the same time steely and unaffected—a theme for a benevolent yet steadfast mission. [. . .] the theme suggests the relics of Middle-earth's ancient glory," sentiments that cannot possibly be applied to Eshkeri's material.[24] Shore's melody is presented as a "fully realized hero's theme,"[25] whereas Eshkeri's cue is intended to evoke ideas of sea shanties (hence the use of a compound time signature). The undulating phrases of Eshkeri's melody are designed to reflect the movement of the sky ship through the air, and the accompanying moto-perpetuo arpeggio quavers generate a sense of forward propulsion that injects the "Boat" theme with an energy not found in Shore's cue. Far from being receptive, sympathetic, steely, unaffected, benevolent or steadfast (to use Adams's descriptors), the *Stardust* cue presents the happy-go-lucky, fun and, at times, comedic life of all those aboard the Caspartine, and is the most unashamedly lively material in the whole score.

The "Boat" and "Pirate" leitmotifs can also be considered with regard to the scores for the various *Pirates of the Caribbean* films, there being an obvious character-type connection with these parts of *Stardust*. Several cues in the scores for the first two *Pirates* films (by Klaus Badelt and Hans Zimmer respectively) feature compound time signatures and continuous pulsing quavers, features that are also found in Eshkeri's cues.[26] However, the use of compound time signatures for pirates is a long-established musical trope—the opening songs for the pirate chorus in Gilbert and Sullivan's 1879 comic opera *The Pirates of Penzance* are both in ⁶⁄₈, for instance[27]—and both of these rhythmic devices are commonly understood as standard features of sea shanties and stereotypical pirate melodies.

Conclusion

The embedding of appropriate filmic codes and adherence to the specific requirements of the genre(s) to which a film is attached inevitably leads to elements of comparison between film scores. For all of the perceived similarities between the scores for *Stardust* and other contemporary fantasy features, the music features a large number of Eshkeri's stylistic hallmarks and has its own unique identity. The principal influence on the score appears to be the composer's training in the Kamen tradition, and although that has not necessarily led directly to Eshkeri's use of leitmotif, it has clearly played a significant role in defining the overall sound of *Stardust*. Despite the high quality of his industry training, Eshkeri was still relatively inexperienced as a film composer when Vaughn approached him about writing this score. He was faced with the challenge of creating music that not only gained Vaughn's approval, but also met the requirements of a contemporary fantasy score, in addition to maintaining its own identity. Eshkeri was not helped in this complex task by the political circumstances surrounding his appointment onto *Stardust*, though the faith shown in him by Vaughn throughout the film's production period meant that he was able to engage with the creative team and develop an understanding of the director's approach to and interpretation of the narrative. Once engaged on the project the time available for the composition of the score was further reduced by aspects of film production that were beyond Eshkeri's control. The archival materials show that although he continued to work on the score across the early months of 2007, several cues were necessarily composed very late in the music-production period. In spite of these difficulties, a consistent tone is maintained across the score owing to the extensive web of leitmotifs.

Stardust demonstrates Eshkeri's ability to combine the expected elements of a contemporary fantasy score (as outlined by Douglas, above) with his personal stylistic fingerprints. The resulting synthesis is a score that can be related to other fantasy features while also establishing itself within that canon of works. Perhaps surprisingly, Eshkeri asserts that the music for *The Lord of the Rings* was never mentioned in any of the discussions he had with Vaughn regarding the sound of *Stardust*.[28] In stark contrast to the film production team, several of whom have commented on the need to differentiate their film visually from those of Peter Jackson,[29] the composer never felt that he was working in the shadow of Howard

Shore, nor that any acknowledgement of Shore's music was required in the creation of his own. As has been demonstrated in the above analysis, instances of similarity between Eshkeri's score for *Stardust* and the music for other fantasy films results from the use of existing musical tropes and established film-music codes rather than any attempt to relate it to other contemporary works. Eshkeri identifies his score with those of his mentors, and it has already been observed that a number of features typical of Michael Kamen's music can be readily identified in Eshkeri's. *Stardust* certainly contains echoes of Kamen's *Back to Gaya*, the score that Eshkeri helped to complete following the composer's death, though the similar orchestral textures and instrumentational choices are housed within vastly contrasting structural frameworks.

There appears to be a substantial difference between the significance of the music for *The Lord of the Rings* as perceived by audiences, and as experienced by composers. Whereas film-goers tend to view Shore's score as a milestone in contemporary fantasy music, this view seems to run counter to the reality for composers working within the industry, for whom this score is not necessarily any more or less important than any other. This gap between perception and process is important because it means that in many cases it is not composers but audiences (and beyond them critics, and even scholars) who infer references to other scores where none exist. While audience perceptions of intertextual references to films including *The Lord of the Rings* and *Pirates of the Caribbean* doubtless strengthen Eshkeri's score, it is his understanding of Vaughn's directorial vision and his extensive and intelligent use of leitmotif that embeds the music as an essential component of the filmic narrative. Perhaps the most remarkable aspect of Eshkeri's score for *Stardust* is that it demonstrates his thorough understanding of the delicate balances inherent in the industry, even though it was his first large-scale film project. Despite being a young composer he was not overawed by the challenges that faced him, and *Stardust* is a testament to his (and Vaughn's) confidence in his training and ability.

Further evidence of the quality and originality of the score can be found in its reuse in television programs and adverts, and music from *Stardust* has appeared in several episodes of the British motoring program *Top Gear*. The first such use was two short excerpts from each of the "Lamia's Inn" sequence and the "Septimus" theme during a feature on the British twenty-four-hour endurance race, in a broadcast on 9 December 2007.[30] Part of 7M69 "Voodoo Doll" accompanied a feature comparing the BMW M3, Mercedes C63 AMG, and Audi RS4 a fortnight later, with further excerpts included every season since 2009.[31] That the first of these television appearances occurred just two months after the film was released in the UK, and while it was still playing in some cinemas, demonstrates the instant impact and appeal of the score; that the producers of *Top Gear* continue to draw on *Stardust* five years after its release is testament to its originality and establishment in the canon of fantasy film scores. The brewer Heineken used a cut of 7M76/77 "Coronation Parts 1 & 2" as the music for their 2010 *Honours* television advert for Strongbow cider. The advert is set in a large hall and shows large crowds of people watching the ceremony, mimicking the equivalent scene from *Stardust*. Eshkeri's cue amplifies the majesty of the sequence, particularly through the intertextual references to the film's coronation evoked by the combination of the advert's visual and aural components.

Paramount may initially have had reservations about commissioning Eshkeri to write the score for *Stardust*, but the quality and appropriateness of the music he composed for the film cannot be doubted. It is in the delicate balance of invention and imitation that a score is defined in the contemporary film-music industry, and unquestionably Eshkeri's *Stardust* meets these requirements. It offers an abundance of the former with just enough of the latter to meet the expectations of the filmmakers, studio and the wider public, and has deservedly become fully established in the canon of contemporary fantasy-film scores.

NOTES

Chapter 1

1. Phil Sutcliffe, "Instrumental to the Film," *Leeds Alumni Magazine* 11 (Summer 2012): 15.

2. Ilan Eshkeri, interviewed by author, 13 September 2007.

3. John Mansell, "Interview with Ilan Eshkeri," *Soundtrack: The Cinemascore and Soundtrack Archives* 2001, www.runmovies.eu/index.php?option=com_content& view=article&id=617:ilan-eshkeri&catid=35:interviews (15 April 2012); Marie-Lise Van Wassenhove, "Interview with Ilan Eshkeri," *Filmmuziek.be* 2004, www.filmmuziek.be/features.cgi?go=detail&id=62 (5 April 2012).

4. Eshkeri, interviewed by author, 13 September 2007.

5. Eshkeri, interviewed by author, 13 September 2007.

6. Eshkeri, interviewed by author, 13 September 2007.

7. The requirements of Eshkeri's joint honours degree programme prohibited him from taking both composition and music technology in his final year.

8. Sutcliffe, "Instrumental to the Film," 15.

9. Ilan Eshkeri, interviewed by author, 8 February 2012.

10. Advances in score production software since the start of the twenty-first century have impacted significantly on the role of the copyist according to Vic Fraser (Vic Fraser, interviewed by author, 21 March 2012). As processed scores have taken over from hand-written scores as the industry norm, so the copyist has had less actual copying (from score to parts) to carry out, and more tidying up and management of presentation to do instead. Although the role of 'copyist' or 'music copyist' still exists on some projects, it is equivalent to (and interchangeable with) 'music preparation,' 'score preparation,' and other, similar titles.

11. Eshkeri, interviewed by author, 13 September 2007.

12. Eshkeri, interviewed by author, 8 February 2012.

13. Eshkeri, interviewed by author, 8 February 2012.

14. Eshkeri, interviewed by author, 8 February 2012.

15. Eshkeri, interviewed by author, 8 February 2012.

16. Ilan Eshkeri in Iain Blair, "From the Bard to the Bean without missing a beat," *Variety* 16 November 2011, www.variety.com/article/VR1118045841?refcatid=13 (16 October 2012).

17. Phil Blanckley, "*Coriolanus*," *Static Mass Emporium: The Essence of Film* 4 June 2012, http://staticmass.net/soundtracks/coriolanus-soundtrack-cd-2011-review/ (16 October 2012).

18. Eshkeri in Blair, "From the Bard to the Bean" (16 October 2012).

19. Ilan Eshkeri, "*Coriolanus*—Ilan Eshkeri Composer Interview," *You-Tube.com* 24 February 2012, www.youtube.com/watch?v=MH5vK4BjCsQ&feature=plcp ([16 October 2012).

20. Blanckley, "*Coriolanus*" (16 October 2012).

21. Ilan Eshkeri, interviewed by author, 21 February 2013.

22. Eshkeri, interviewed by author, 21 February 2013.

23. Laurence E. MacDonald, *The Invisible Art of Film Music: A Comprehensive History* (New York: Arsley House Publishers Inc., 1998), 341 and 359.

24. Miguel Mera, *Mychael Danna's* The Ice Storm: *A Film Score Guide* (Lanham, MD.: Scarecrow Press, 2007), 5–6.

25. Trevor Jones in David Cooper and Christopher Fox, "Keynote Interview with Trevor Jones," in *CineMusic? Constructing the Film Score*, eds. David Cooper, Christopher Fox and Ian Sapiro (Newcastle-upon-Tyne: Cambridge Scholars Publishing, 2008), 1.

26. Eshkeri, interviewed by author, 13 September 2007.

27. See, for instance, "Open Range," *Filmtracks: Modern Soundtrack Reviews* 2003, rev. 2009, www.filmtracks.com/titles/open_range.html (4 April 2012), and "Open Range—Trivia," *Internet Movie Database* 2012, www.imdb.com/title/tt0316356/trivia (4 April 2012).

28. Eshkeri, interviewed by author, 8 February 2012.

29. Unlike the majority of film composers, Kamen would routinely do some of his own orchestration, working as sole orchestrator or a member of an orchestration team on nearly thirty of the eighty film and television projects he undertook as composer. He also conducted a similar proportion of his film scores. For a full credit list see "Michael Kamen," *Internet Movie Database* 2012, www.imdb.com/name/nm0004383 (4 April 2012).

30. A look through the music teams for the films of Ed Shearmur reveals that McLaughlin, Fraser, Elhai and Brown were also involved with a number of his film scores, notably *The Wings of the Dove* (1997), *Jakob the Liar* (1999), *The Count of Monte Cristo* (2002), *Reign of Fire* (2002), *Johnny English* (2003), *Sky Captain and the World of Tomorrow* (2004), and *Derailed* (2005), the music department for each of which includes at least three of these professionals.

31. Eshkeri, interviewed by author, 8 February 2012.

32. Tilman Remme in "A Composer's Story: Making the Music for *Colosseum*," special feature on *Colosseum: A Gladiator's Story*, dir. Tilman Remme, BBC Video, 2003 [DVD] (0:01:44–0:01:48).

33. Remme in "A Composer's Story" (0:01:48–0:01:52).

34. Eshkeri, interviewed by author, 8 February 2012.

35. Remme in "A Composer's Story" (0:02:02–0:02:40).

36. Ilan Eshkeri in "A Composer's Story: Making the Music for *Colosseum*," special feature on *Colosseum: A Gladiator's Story*, dir. Tilman Remme, BBC Video, 2003 [DVD] (0:02:49–0:02:51).

37. Eshkeri in "A Composer's Story" (0:03:04–0:03:09). Several figures for the size of the orchestra are quoted in this mini documentary ranging from forty up to sixty.

38. "A Composer's Story" (0:03:43–0:03:49 and 0:04:10–0:04:18).

39. Eshkeri in "A Composer's Story" (0:06:34–0:06:50).

40. Steve McLaughlin in Mikael Carlsson, "Mr Kamen's Final Opus: An interview with Steve McLaughlin, Christopher Brooks and Robert Elhai," liner notes to Michael Kamen, *Back to Gaya: Original Motion Picture Soundtrack* (Moviescore Media, Sweden, 2012), 2.

41. Christopher Brooks describes the additional composers as "more arrangers on this project than composers." Brooks in Carlsson, "Mr Kamen's Final Opus," 3.

42. Michael Kamen, *Back to Gaya: Original Motion Picture Soundtrack* (Moviescore Media, Sweden, 2012).

43. Eshkeri, interviewed by author, 8 February 2012.

44. Eshkeri, interviewed by author, 8 February 2012.

45. Van Wassenhove, "Interview with Ilan Eshkeri" (5 April 2012).

46. Various Artists, *Layer Cake* (London: EMI, 2004).

47. 2007 was only the second year of this award, which was renamed "Breakout Composer of the Year" in 2008. With hindsight, this would really have been a more apt title for the award when won by Eshkeri.

48. According to the Broadcasters' Audience Research Board (BARB), 6.437 million viewers saw the programme when it was first aired on Channel 4, with a further 2.333 million watching the re-run the following day. A further 707,000 saw the first airing one hour later, on Channel 4+1. Based purely on figures for the first airing on Channel 4, *The Snowman and the Snowdog* was the second most viewed programme on the channel in 2012 behind the opening ceremony for the London Paralympic Games, and ahead of the Paralympic closing ceremony. Figures taken from various pages on *BARB* 2013, www.barb.co.uk/ (10 January 2013).

49. The other *Variety* articles in the series were on Ludovic Bource (*The Artist*), Jonsi (*We Bought a Zoo*), Howard Shore (*Hugo*), John Williams (*War Horse* and *The Adventures of Tintin*), Alexandre Desplat (*Harry Potter and the Deathly Hallows Part 2*, among others) and Cliff Martinez (*Drive*). In the event, *Variety* correctly predicted four of the five nominees (Bource, Shore and Williams twice).

50. For more information on AHAE and his photographs, see http://ahae.com.

Chapter 2

1. Ilan Eshkeri, interviewed by author, 8 February 2012.

2. Fred Karlin and Rayburn Wright, *On the Track*, revised 2nd edition (New York: Routledge, 2004), 3.

3. Karlin and Wright, *On the Track*, 3.

4. Dan Carlin Sr., *Music in Film and Video Productions* (London: Focal Press, 1991), 3–4. Italics original.

5. Carlin Sr., *Music in Film and Video Productions*, 56.

6. Richard Davis, *Complete Guide to Film Scoring* (Boston, Mass: Berklee Press, 1999), 78.

7. George Fenton in Ian Sapiro, Scoring the Score: The Role of the Orchestrator in the Contemporary British Film Industry. Diss., University of Leeds, 2011, 153.

8. Accounts vary as to precisely when digital picture editing became the industry norm, since the transition occurred gradually over a period of years in the late 1980s and 1990s. Mervyn Cooke and Dan Carlin Jr. both assert that editing became computer-based in the 1980s, whereas Richard Davis and film editor Dede Allen both place it in the early 1990s, and Michael Allen suggests it happened "in the 1990s." See Mervyn Cooke, *A History of Film Music* (Cambridge: Cambridge University Press, 2008), 57; Dan Carlin Jr. quoted in Vincent LoBrutto, *Sound-on-Film: Interviews with Creators of Film Sound* (Westport, Conn.: Praeger Publishers, 1994), 109; Davis, *Complete Guide to Film Scoring*, 77; Ric Gentry and Dede Allen, "An Interview with Dede Allen," *Film Quarterly* 46, no. 1 (Autumn 1992): 12–22 passim; Michael Allen, "From *Bwana Devil* to *Batman Forever*: Technology in Contemporary Hollywood Cinema," in *Contemporary Hollywood Cinema*, eds. Steve Neale and Murray Smith (London: Routledge, 2004), 122. For a detailed account of the development of picture editing technology and its impact on the creation of music in the contemporary film industry see Sapiro, Scoring the Score, 149–59.

9. Karlin and Wright, *On the Track*, 33.

10. Hans Zimmer, quoted in Matt Hurwitz, "Scoring for Picture: Hans Zimmer's Scoring Collective—Composer Collaboration at Remote Control Productions," in *The Routledge Film Music Source Book*, eds. James Wierzbicki, Nathan Platte and Colin Roust (New York: Routledge, [2007] 2012), 256.

11. Vera John-Steiner, *Creative Collaboration* (Oxford: Oxford University Press, 2000), 85.

12. For discussion of the use of temp tracks see, for instance, Karlin and Wright, *On the Track*; Ron Sadoff, "The role of the music editor and the 'temp track' as blueprint for the score, source music, and scource music of films," *Popular Music* 25, no. 2 (2006): 165–83.

13. Eshkeri, interviewed by author, 8 February 2012.

14. Film trailers are not usually created and distributed by the film production companies, but are outsourced to other companies that specialize in these products. Accordingly, while trailer music may influence public perceptions of film sound, it is unlikely to have significant impact on composers of film music. The music used in the theatrical trailer for *Stardust* will be discussed in detail in Chapter 3.

15. Ilan Eshkeri, interviewed by author, 13 September 2007.

16. Eshkeri, interviewed by author, 13 September 2007.

17. Each cue is identified using a three-part code. The initial number represents the reel of film, the M shows it is a music cue, and the final number is the

order of the cue within the entire film. Historical convention returns the final number to 1 at the start of each reel, meaning that it represents the order of the cue within its reel, but Eshkeri prefers to number his cues continuously through a film, since this makes it simpler if a cue moves from one reel to another (as happened in this film). These cues are therefore: reel 4, music, cue 34; reel 6, music, cue 67; and reel 7, music, cue 73.

18. Arnold Whittall, "Leitmotif," *Grove Music Online. Oxford Music Online* 2012, http://0-www.oxfordmusiconline.com.wam.leeds.ac.uk/subscriber/article/grove/music/16360 (21 November 2012).

19. Theodore Adorno and Hans Eisler, *Composing for the Films.* 2nd edition (London: Continuum, [1947] 2005), 5.

20. Gorbman, *Unheard Melodies: Narrative Film Music* (Bloomington, Ind.: Indiana University Press, 1987), 90.

21. Irena Paulus, "Williams versus Wagner or an Attempt at Linking Music Epics," *International Review of the Aesthetics and Sociology of Music* 31, no. 2 (2000): 157.

22. The relative lack of thematic development in the music for *Johnny English Reborn* mirrors the generally low level of motivic development in scores for pre-*Casino Royale* James Bond films, further reinforcing parallels between the two protagonists.

23. Transcription by author.

24. In the case of *Stardust* the basis of the tone-semitone octatonic scale as the first four pitches of minor scales a tritone apart is also significant. See the discussion of Eshkeri's music for Lamia and the witches in Chapter 5.

25. "*The Young Victoria*: Production Notes" (GK Films, LLC, 2008), 15.

26. Rather than Schubert's original song, the film features Lizst's piano transcription of "Ständchen." This is a small anachronism, since it is first heard in the cross-cut scenes described by O'Sullivan in the following quotation; these are set in 1836, the year of Victoria's ascension to the throne, but Liszt did not transcribe the song until 1837. See Alan Walker, Maria Eckhardt, and Rena Charnin Mueller, "Liszt, Franz," *Grove Music Online. Oxford Music Online* 2012, http://0-www.oxfordmusiconline.com.wam.leeds.ac.uk/subscriber/article/grove/music/48265pg28 (26 November 2012).

27. Denis O'Sullivan, quoted in "*The Young Victoria*: Production Notes," 15.

28. This *Slavonic Dance* is numbered 3 in the original two-piano version, and 6 in Dvořák's own published orchestrations. Since the material heard in the film is orchestral, it is referred to here as Op. 46 No. 6. See Antonín Dvořák, *Slavonic Dances* Op. 46 (Prague: Státní nakladatelství krásné literatury, [1878] 1955). The "Galop Infernal" starts at bar 87 in musical number 15 of *Orphée aux Enfers*. See Jacques Offenbach, *Orphée aux Enfers* (Berlin: Bote & Bock, [1858] 1999).

29. Matthew Vaughn, "Commentary with writers Matthew Vaughn and Jane Goldman," *Stardust*, dir. Matthew Vaughn, Paramount Pictures, 2007 [Blu-ray 2009] (1:14:58–1:15:02).

30. The music that precedes the *Slavonic Dance*, 5M45A "Pirate Montage," was written very early in the production process, before the point at which the Dvořák work was selected for inclusion in the scene. As a result, more changes were made to the *Slavonic Dance* than might normally be expected of a piece of pre-existing music.

31. Daryl Kell, interviewed by author, 19 March 2012.

32. Anahid Kassabian, *Hearing Film: Tracking Identifications in Contemporary Hollywood Film Music* (New York: Routledge, 2001), 49.

33. Jeff Smith, *The Sounds of Commerce: Marketing Popular Film Music* (New York: Columbia University Press, 1998), 155.

34. Smith, *The Sounds of Commerce*, 155.

35. J. Peter Burkholder, "Quotation," *Grove Music Online. Oxford Music Online* 2012, http://0-www.oxfordmusiconline.com.wam.leeds.ac.uk/subscriber/article/grove/music/52854 (27 November 2012).

36. J. Peter Burkholder, "Allusion," *Grove Music Online. Oxford Music Online* 2012, http://0-www.oxfordmusiconline.com.wam.leeds.ac.uk/subscriber/article/grove/music/52852 (27 November 2012).

37. Kassabian, *Hearing Film*, 50; Burkholder, "Allusion" (27 November 2012).

38. Eshkeri, interviewed by author, 13 September 2007.

39. The melody actually predates the nursery rhyme considerably and is of French origin. *Ah! Vous dirai-je, Maman* dates from 1761 and has also been used in pieces of classical music including a set of keyboard variations by Mozart, a copy of which is kept by Eshkeri tucked into the back of the printed *Stardust* score. Although most viewers of the film will only associate the tune with the nursery rhyme, this additional knowledge of its history and use adds to the intertextual web of meaning inherent in the score.

40. Ilan Eshkeri, interviewed by author, 12 September 2012.

41. Eshkeri, interviewed by author, 12 September 2012.

42. Translated by author.

43. See Bill Wrobel, "Self-Borrowing in the Music of Bernard Herrmann," *Journal of Film Music* 2 (2003): 249–71.

44. David Cooper, *Bernard Herrmann's* The Ghost and Mrs. Muir: *A Film Score Guide* (Lanham, Md.: Scarecrow Press, 2005), 74–76.

45. Ben Winters, *Erich Wolfgang Korngold's* The Adventures of Robin Hood: *A Film Score Guide* (Lanham, Md.: Scarecrow Press, 2007), 38–49.

46. The composer actually had very little time to compose and record all of the music for the final reel of the film.

47. "Coronation Parts 1 & 2" accompanies the crowning of Tristan and Yvaine and the start of their reign over Stormhold; "Todesfinale" is heard over the deaths of the protagonists in *Ring of the Nibelungs*, following which it is observed that "today the old gods will die with them." *Ring of the Nibelungs*, dir. Uli Edel, Tandem Communications, 2004 (2:52:05–2:52:07).

48. *Stardust's* "magic" music is discussed in Chapter 3.

49. "A sweetener is any effect that is not recorded with the original track, but added later." See Earle Hagen, *Scoring for Films*, updated edition (Los Angeles: Alfred Publishing Co., Inc., 1971), 153. Hagen refers specifically to live sounds recorded separately to the main recording sessions, but in the contemporary industry sweeteners also include sampled sounds which might be added to the live recorded sound. Sweetening is the process of combining these additional sounds and the recorded music. See also George Burt, *The Art of Film Music: Special Emphasis on Hugo Friedhofer, Alex North, David Raksin, Leonard Rosenman* (Boston, Mass: Northeastern University Press, 1994), 244.

50. Kell, interviewed by author, 19 March 2012.

51. Eshkeri, interviewed by author, 8 February 2012.

52. Karlin and Wright, *On the Track*, 5.

53. Eshkeri, interviewed by author, 8 February 2012.

54. The *Canon* is the first, more famous section of a two-part work, *Canon and Gigue in D*, by the German Baroque composer, Johann Pachelbel.

55. Eshkeri, interviewed by author, 8 February 2012.

56. The R at the end of the cue number identifies it as a revision. Most of the cues in the film went through several versions before receiving directorial approval, but those specifically marked with R show that previous versions received approval, and revisions were made subsequent to that point.

57. Eshkeri, interviewed by author, 8 February 2012.

58. Vaughn, "Commentary with writers Matthew Vaughn and Jane Goldman," (1:28:30).

59. Vaughn also approached Take That to create a song for *X-Men: First Class* (2011), the result of which is *Love, Love*. See Michael Leader, "Matthew Vaughn interview: *X-Men: First Class, Thor*, Hollywood, James Bond, Take That and more," *Den of Geek* 2011, www.denofgeek.com/movies/james-bond/17507/matthew-vaughn-interview-x-men-first-class-thor-hollywood-james-bond-take-that-and-more (30 November 2012).

60. Ian Inglis, "Introduction: Popular Music and Film," in *Popular Music and Film*, ed. Ian Inglis (London: Wallflower Press, 2003), 3.

61. Sadoff, "The role of the music editor and the 'temp track' as blueprint for the score, source music, and scource music of films," 182 n. 34.

62. Sadoff's consideration relates to films with predominantly orchestral scores rather than those like *Saturday Night Fever* (dir. John Badham. Robert Stigwood Organisation, 1977), which features a number of songs written specifically for the film by the Bee Gees within a popular music soundtrack.

63. Lee Barron, "'Music Inspired By...': The Curious Case of the Missing Soundtrack," in *Popular Music and Film*, ed. Ian Inglis (London: Wallflower Press, 2003), 150.

64. For further information on synergy in the film and music industries see Jeff Smith, *The Sounds of Commerce* (New York: Columbia University Press, 1998), 24 passim.

65. Vaughn, "Commentary with writers Matthew Vaughn and Jane Goldman," (2:00:38).

66. Richard Lancaster, interviewed by author, 3 May 2012.

Chapter 3

1. World Fantasy Board, "1991 World Fantasy Award Winners and Nominees," *World Fantasy Convention* 1991, www.worldfantasy.org/awards/1991.html (7 December 2012).

2. Anthony Breznican, "Storyteller Gaiman wishes upon a star: Movie magic touches his fairy tale *Stardust*," *USA Today*, 31 July 2007, 1D. Available online at

http://usatoday30.usatoday.com/printedition/life/20070731/d_cover31.art.htm (30 November 2012).

3. Neil Gaiman, "The Quest for the Stone...," special feature on *Stardust*, dir. Matthew Vaughn, Paramount Pictures, 2007 [Blu-ray 2009].

4. Mythopoeic Society, "Mythopoeic Awards: Winners," *Mythopoeic Society* 2012, www.mythsoc.org/awards/winners/ (30 November 2012).

5. Young Library Adult Services Association, "Alex Awards—2000 Selection(s)," *American Literary Association* 2000, www.ala.org/awardsgrants/awards/231/winners/2000 (30 November 2012).

6. Gaiman does not specify a precise year, but offers information on contemporaneous literary and scientific events that places the start of the narrative between 1836 and 1840.

7. Neil Gaiman, *Stardust* (London: Headline Publishing Group, 2005), 29.

8. Alice Curry argues that Tristran's world-view at the start of *Stardust* is shaped by "an Orientalist discourse," and it is therefore "no coincidence that the star [. . .] falls to the East." See Alice Curry, "'The pale trees shook, although no wind blew, and it seemed to Tristran that they shook in anger': 'blind space' and ecofeminism in a post-colonial reading of Neil Gaiman and Charles Vess's graphic novel *Stardust* (1998)," *Barnboken—Journal of Children's Literature Research* 33, no. 2 (2010): 24. For further information on Orientalism in literature see Edward W. Saïd, *Orientalism* (London: Routledge and Kegan Paul, 1978).

9. Gaiman, *Stardust*, 59.

10. Tertius has already been poisoned by Septimus, who has himself been misled by Primus and set out after his oldest brother in the wrong direction.

11. Derek Paget, "Speaking Out: The Transformations of *Trainspotting*," in *Adaptations: From Text to Screen, Screen to Text*, eds. Deborah Cartmell and Imelda Whelehan (New York: Routledge, 1999), 131.

12. Brian McFarlane, "Reading Film and Literature," in *The Cambridge Companion to Literary Adaptation*, eds. Deborah Cartmell and Imelda Whelehan (Cambridge: Cambridge University Press, 2007), 16.

13. McFarlane, "Reading Film and Literature," 16.

14. McFarlane, "Reading Film and Literature," 15. Italics original.

15. The separation of the author's intent from the meaning of a text was a key concern of the poststructuralist movement in the 1970s, particularly Frenchmen such as Barthes and Foucault. See, for instance, Roland Barthes, "The Death of the Author," in *Image–Music–Text*, ed. and trans. Stephen Heath (New York: Hill, 1977), 142–48; Michael Foucault, "What is an Author?," in *The Foucault Reader: An Introduction to Foucault's Thought*, ed. Paul Rabinow (London: Penguin Books, 1984), 101–20.

16. Deborah Cartmell, "Text to Screen: Introduction," in *Adaptations: From Text to Screen, Screen to Text*, eds. Deborah Cartmell and Imelda Whelehan (New York: Routledge, 1999), 28.

17. Alison Flood, "Neil Gaiman wins Carnegie Medal," *Guardian.co.uk* 24 June 2010, www.guardian.co.uk/books/2010/jun/24/neil-gaiman-carnegie-graveyard-book (30 November 2012).

18. Breznican, "Storyteller Gaiman wishes upon a star" (30 November 2012).

19. Capone, "Capone talks to Matthew Vaughn about *Stardust*, Bobby De Niro, *X-Men*, *Thor* and much more!!!," *Aint it Cool News* 2007, www.aintitcool.com/node/33607 (30 November 2012).

20. MTV, "*Stardust* Author Neil Gaiman Tells Why He Turns Down Most Adaptations—But Not This One," *MTV* 2007. www.mtv.com/news/articles/1566862/neil-gaiman-makes-his-stardust.jhtml (30 November 2012).

21. Rob Carnevale, "*Stardust*—Matthew Vaughn and Neil Gaiman interview," *IndieLondon*, www.indielondon.co.uk/Film-Review/stardust-matthew-vaughn-and-neil-gaiman-interview (30 November 2012).

22. Emanuel Levy, "Interviews: Stardust with Matthew Vaughn," *Emanuel Levy*, www.emanuellevy.com/interview/stardust-with-matthew-vaughn-2/ (30 November 2012).

23. MTV, "*Stardust* Author Neil Gaiman Tells Why He Turns Down Most Adaptations—But Not This One" (30 November 2012).

24. Levy, "Interviews: Stardust with Matthew Vaughn" (30 November 2012).

25. Dave McNary and Nicole Laporte, "Par sprinkles *Stardust*: Vaughn to adapt, helm Gaiman novel," *Variety* 2005, www.variety.com/article/VR1117931609 (30 November 2012).

26. Gaiman, "The Quest for the Stone..."

27. Matthew Vaughn, quoted in Edward Douglas, "Exclusive: *Stardust* director Matthew Vaughn," *SuperHeroHype* 2007, www.superherohype.com/features/articles/94533-exclusive-stardust-director-matthew-vaughn (30 November 2012).

28. John Hiscock, "Matthew Vaughn: The Brit who's making the stars shine," *The Telegraph* 5 October 2007, www.telegraph.co.uk/culture/film/starsandstories/3668336/Matthew-Vaughn-The-Brit-whos-making-the-stars-shine.html (30 November 2012).

29. Levy, "Interviews: Stardust with Matthew Vaughn" (30 November 2012).

30. MTV, "*Stardust* Author Neil Gaiman Tells Why He Turns Down Most Adaptations—But Not This One" (30 November 2012).

31. Michael Fleming, "Starry cast for *Stardust*: Thesps align for Vaughn-helmed Gaiman adaptation," *Variety* 2006, www.variety.com/article/VR1117939318 (30 November 2012).

32. Breznican, "Storyteller Gaiman wishes upon a star" (30 November 2012).

33. Matthew Vaughn, "A Portal to Another World...," special feature on *Stardust*, dir. Matthew Vaughn, Paramount Pictures, 2007 [Blu-ray 2009].

34. Use of Tristran/Tristan is retained in the following discussion when considering the character in the book and film respectively.

35. Gaiman, *Stardust*. The description of Tristran and Victoria witnessing the star falling starts on page 37, with the witches only finally articulating that they have identified the same event on page 54.

36. Matthew Vaughn, "Commentary with Matthew Vaughn and Jane Goldman," *Stardust*, dir. Matthew Vaughn, Paramount Pictures, 2007 [Blu-ray 2009] (0:14:39–0:14:46)

37. Secundus's music is considered in detail in Chapter 5.

38. Gaiman, *Stardust*, 145.

39. Gaiman, *Stardust*, 145.

40. Susan Cahill considers some of the implications arising from the use of these names in "Through the Looking Glass: Fairy-Tale Cinema and the Spectacle of Femininity in *Stardust* and *The Brothers Grimm*," *Marvels & Tales* 24, no. 1 (2010): 60–61.

41. Gaiman, *Stardust*, 158.

42. *Stardust*, dir. Matthew Vaughn, Paramount Pictures, 2007 [Blu-ray 2009] (00:38:17–00:38:51).

43. Throughout the film Lamia and the princes use rune stones to locate the star/necklace. Septimus presumably uses them to know to where he is headed for the finale, but this is not shown in the film and his reactions at the gap in the wall do not reinforce this theory. In any case, Tristan does not have, and would not have known how to read rune stones.

44. Vaughn, "A Portal to Another World…"

45. Gaiman, *Stardust*, 162–63.

46. Marcin Rusnak argues that the result of rewriting *Stardust*'s third act is that the filmmakers "exchanged one thing for another—in this case meaning for action," citing the removal of the witch queen's self-inflicted failure as one such lost layer of meaning. See Marcin Rusnak, "Blessings and curses of the silver screen: Film adaptations of *Coraline* and *Stardust* by Neil Gaiman," in *Alternate Life-Worlds in Literary Fiction*, edited by Ewa Kębłowska-Ławniczak, Zdzisław Wąsik and Teresa Bruś (Wrocław: Wyższa Szkoła Filologiczna we Wrocławiu, 2011), 144.

47. In the novel Una is released from Sal's service by a complicated conjunction of events which includes there being two Mondays in a week. Victoria Forester is given Tristran's blessing to marry Robert Monday which brings this part of the requirement to fruition; had Tristran continued with his original plan to marry Victoria the Lady Una, who it is later revealed is Tristran's mother, would never have left Sal's service.

48. The manner of Lamia's death can be related to Rusnik's criticism of the film's third act (see note 46). Rather than merely deny herself the chance to capture the star, by releasing and reuniting Tristan and Yvaine the witch is the architect of her own death. Far from exchanging meaning for action, the filmmakers substitute one meaning for another within an action scene.

49. The visuals show each ghost reduced to a speck of light which floats up to heaven, apart from Septimus, whose speck descends to hell. Goldman and Vaughn draw attention to this final consideration of Septimus's character on their Blu-ray commentary.

50. Gaiman, *Stardust*, 189; *Stardust*, dir. Matthew Vaughn [Blu-ray 2009] (2:00:07–2:00:20)

51. Matthew Vaughn, "Have You Seen a Fallen Star?," special feature on *Stardust*, dir. Matthew Vaughn, Paramount Pictures, 2007 [Blu-ray 2009].

52. Steve McLaughlin, interviewed by author, 8 February 2012.

53. Filming ran across seventy-seven days from 25 April to 19 September, 2006. See Stephen Jones, Stardust: *The Visual Companion* (London: Titan Books, 2007), 36 and 148.

54. The fan site was at www.kryptonfan.com but no longer exists. The podcast is still available at http://chuckr7.hipcast.com/deluge/3adea8c1-5dd3-38cf-3dba-9df262e2f06e.mp3 (8 January 2013).

55. John Ottman, interviewed by Chuck R, "Episode 53," podcast, *Krypton Fan* 2006, http://chuckr7.hipcast.com/deluge/3adea8c1-5dd3-38cf-3dba-9df262e2f06e.mp3 (8 January 2013). The comments on *Stardust* are at 00.23.37–00.23.46.

56. Laura M. Holsen and Sharon Waxman. "A Shuffle at Paramount and more to come," *New York Times* 11 January 2007, www.nytimes.com/2007/01/11/business/media/11studio.html?scp=1&sq=paramount&st=nyt&_r=0 (5 December 2012); Laura M. Holsen and Sharon Waxman, "Turmoil continues at Paramount Pictures as president resigns," *New York Times* 11 January 2007, www.nytimes.com/2007/01/11/technology/11iht-studio.4169382.html?_r=0 (5 December 2012).

57. Personal communication with author, 27 February 2013.

58. McLaughlin, interviewed by author, 8 February 2012.

59. Moriarty, "Moriarty Visits London For A Dash Of *Stardust*! Part One Of Two!!," *Aint it Cool News* 21 July 2006, www.aintitcool.com/node/23933 (8 January 2013).

60. By contrast, the trailers for *The Lord of the Rings: The Fellowship of the Ring*, *Pirates of the Caribbean: Curse of the Black Pearl*, and *The Chronicles of Narnia: The Lion, the Witch and the Wardrobe* each used four sources. See "Trailer Music," SoundTrack.Net 2013, www.soundtrack.net/trailers/ (11 January 2013).

61. Quint, "Quint wanders around Pinewood and checks out Matthew Vaughn's *Stardust*!!!" *Aint it Cool News* 7 July 2006, www.aintitcool.com/node/23785 (8 January 2013).

62. Matthew Vaughn, "A Portal to Another World..."

63. Matthew Vaughn, "A Portal to Another World..."

64. Lorenzo Di Bonaventura, "A Quest of Enormous Importance...," special feature on *Stardust*, dir. Matthew Vaughn, Paramount Pictures, 2007 [Blu-ray 2009].

65. Angela Wampler, "*Stardust* — 'It's *Pirates Of The Caribbean* Meets *The Princess Bride*,'" *A! Magazine for the Arts* 29 May 2007, http://artsmagazine.info/articles.php?view=detail&id=07052920161174501 (8 January 2013).

66. Quint, "Quint wanders around Pinewood and checks out Matthew Vaughn's *Stardust*!!!" (8 January 2013).

67. See Jones, Stardust: *The Visual Companion*, 58–59.

68. Jane Goldman, "Commentary with Matthew Vaughn and Jane Goldman," *Stardust*, dir. Matthew Vaughn, Paramount Pictures, 2007 [Blu-ray 2009] (2:00:27). Vaughn agrees with Goldman's assertion, replying "exactly."

Chapter 4

1. The shooting script for *Stardust* is included in Stardust*: The Visual Companion*, and differs from the dialogue heard in the film in several places. See Stephen Jones, Stardust*: The Visual Companion* (London: Titan Books, 2007), 162–240.

2. See Ian Sapiro, Scoring the Score: The Role of the Orchestrator in the Contemporary British Film Industry. Diss., University of Leeds, 2011, 211.

3. See Sapiro, Scoring the Score, 203–14 for more information.

4. Sapiro, Scoring the Score, 209–10.

5. Fred Karlin and Rayburn Wright, *On the Track*, revised 2nd edition (New York: Routledge, 2004). They outline the scoring process on page 3. For other accounts of the film-score production process see also Dan Carlin Sr., *Music in Film and Video Productions* (London: Focal Press, 1991); Richard Davis, *Complete Guide to Film Scoring: The Art and Business of Writing Music for Movies and TV* (Boston, MA: Berklee Press, 1999), 78; Jeff Rona, *The Reel World, Scoring for Pictures; A Practical Guide to the Art, Technology and Business of Composing for Film and Television* (San Francisco: Miller Freeman Books, 2000); Sonny Kompanek, *From Score to Screen: Sequencers, Scores and Second Thoughts: The New Film Scoring Process* (New York: Schirmer Trade Books, 2004).

6. Based on Sapiro, Scoring the Score, 210.

7. Ilan Eshkeri, interviewed by author, 13 September 2007.

8. Scorenotes, "Interview with Ilan Eshkeri," *ScoreNotes* 2007, http://scorenotes.com/interview/eshkeri/ilan_eshkeri.html (15 August 2012).

9. Scorenotes, "Interview with Ilan Eshkeri" (15 August 2012).

10. John Mansell, "Interview with Ilan Eshkeri," *Soundtrack: The Cinemascore and Soundtrack Archives* 2011, http://www.runmovies.eu/index.php?option=com_content&view=article&id=617:ilan-eshkeri&catid=35:interviews (15 August 2012).

11. The use of these melodies and their narrative connotations are considered in detail in Chapter 5.

12. Eshkeri, interviewed by author, 13 September 2007.

13. Scorenotes, "Interview with Ilan Eshkeri" (15 August 2012).

14. The principal *Stardust* themes and motifs, and their connections, are considered in detail in Chapter 5.

15. The musical representation of Lamia and the witches is considered in detail in Chapter 5.

16. Transcription and reduction by author, created from composer's audio demo.

17. Email from Ilan Eshkeri to Steve McLaughlin, 28 January 2007.

18. Marie-Lise Van Wassenhove, "Interview with Ilan Eshkeri," *Filmmuziek.be* 2004, www.filmmuziek.be/features.cgi?go=detail&id=62 (15 August 2012). The PDF of the orchestral score was created on 25 May 2007, the date of the final Stardust recording sessions, so the theme must have been recorded at one of those sessions. It is track 13 "Tristan & Yvaine" on the official soundtrack album.

19. Email from Christoph Bauschinger to Ilan Eshkeri, 28 February 2007.

20. According to Stephen Jones, "following the completion of principal photography, over the next few months visual effects supervisor Peter Chiang and his

team used state-of-the-art computer technology to optically enhance a large number of sequences." Stephen Jones, Stardust: The Visual Companion (London: Titan
Books, 2007), 152. That effects were still being added to the film in February, five
months after shooting was finished, indicates both the scale of the task, and the
ongoing changes that were made to the picture even after Eshkeri had started
work on the score.

21. Steve McLaughlin, interviewed by author, 8 February 2012.

22. In the UK, no more than twenty-four minutes of music may be used
from a three-hour recording session.

23. The reference in the notes to "Tristran" is doubly incorrect—the character's name is altered to Tristan in the film, and in any case this sequence starts at a
point before he is born, and concerns his father, Dunstan.

24. Tristam is clearly a spelling mistake, probably a result of the hurry with
which Bauschinger prepared these notes.

25. Matthew Vaughn, "Commentary with writers Matthew Vaughn and Jane
Goldman," Stardust, dir. Matthew Vaughn, Paramount Pictures, 2007 [Blu-ray
2009] (0:06:46–0:06:57).

26. There were three orchestral line-ups, 'A,' 'B,' and 'C' used on Stardust, the
'A' orchestra being the largest and the 'C' orchestra the smallest. The precise con-
stitution of these ensembles is given in an invoice produced by Andy Brown on 17
May 2007, which contains the following information:

Table 4.4n. Constitution of the three *Stardust* orchestras

Orchestration:															
Strings	A	B	C	Woodwind	A	B	C	Brass	A	B	C	Others	A	B	C
violins 1	14	12	12	flutes	2	1	1	horns	6	4	1	percussion	3	2	1
violins 2	12	12	10	oboes	2	1	1	trumpets	3	1	0	timps	1	1	1
violas	10	8	8	clarinet	1	1	1	tenor trombones	3	2	0	harp	1	1	1
celli	8	8	8	bass clarinet	1	1	0	bass trombones	2	1	0	celeste/piano	1	1	1
double basses	6	6	4	bassoon	1	1	0	tuba	1	0	0				
				contra bassoon	1	1	0								
	50	46	42		8	6	3		15	8	1		6	5	4
Total Musicians:	Orch A: 79 / Orch B: 65 / Orch C: 50														

27. Ilan Eshkeri, interviewed by author, 12 September 2012.

28 The list includes fifty-five pieces of music, but since 2M15A is a fix for
2M15 it is not considered as a separate cue in this count. Similarly, 2M15 and
2M15A are considered as one cue in the total cues for reel 2 shown in table 4.3.

29. Cue 2M13 was excised relatively early in the process, and was no longer
part of the score by April.

30. Vaughn, "Commentary with writers Matthew Vaughn and Jane Goldman," (0:51:38–0:51:49).

31. Email from Steve McLaughlin to Randy Spendlove, 12 March 2007.

32. Andy Brown recalls that although it would have been preferable to record
the whole score in the same space, Abbey Road Studio 1, the Air Lyndhurst Studio was "totally appropriate" for the final Coronation sequence (7M76/77) since it
is a converted church and its cavernous acoustic suited the narrative setting in
which the cue would be heard in the film. Andy Brown, interviewed by author, 23
March 2012.

33. A stem is a submix of part of the orchestra, usually an individual instrumental section such as strings, woodwind, brass or percussion.

34. The results of such an undertaking could not be presented clearly in the available space in a publication of this nature in any case.

Chapter 5

1. *Star Wars* itself draws on techniques developed during the Hollywood studio era, and accordingly Eshkeri's approach can be seen to have its roots in film scores such as *Now, Voyager* (1942), in which Max Steiner sets tonal and chromatic themes in opposition. See Kate Daubney, *Max Steiner's* Now, Voyager: *A Film Score Guide* (Westport, Conn.: Greenwood Press, 2000).

2. Irena Paulus, "Williams versus Wagner or an Attempt at Linking Music Epics," *International Review of the Aesthetics and Sociology of Music* 31, no. 2 (2000): 168.

3. Alice Curry, "'The pale trees shook, although no wind blew, and it seemed to Tristran that they shook in anger': 'blind space' and ecofeminism in a postcolonial reading of Neil Gaiman and Charles Vess's graphic novel *Stardust* (1998)," *Barnboken—Journal of Children's Literature Research* 33, no. 2 (2010): 26.

4. Cues 2M16 and 2M16A are numbered out of sequence, since 2M16A is actually the first of the two. There seems to be no reason for this, since 2M16 clearly cannot ever have been intended to be placed ahead of 2M16A for narrative reasons, and 2M16A could instead have been numbered 2M15B.

5. *Stardust*, dir. Matthew Vaughn. Paramount Pictures, 2007 [Blu-Ray 2009] (1:32:09–1:32:14).

6. The theme appears in both 2M11 and 2M11Alt, though in slightly different rhythmic presentations. 2M11 Alt appears in the film, and is therefore the focus of this consideration.

7. Ilan Eshkeri, interviewed by author, 12 September 2012.

8. A similar example can be sound in George Gershwin's folk opera *Porgy and Bess* (1935). Whereas each of the main male characters, Porgy, Crown, and Sporting Life, has a distinct musical identity, Bess is not allocated her own theme. Her relationships with the three men run across the story and tie the narrative together, and she is defined throughout the opera by the musical persona of whichever male she is with at the time. See Joseph P. Swain, *The Broadway Musical: A Critical and Musical Survey* (New York: Oxford University Press, 1990), 62.

9. Susan Cahill discusses Yvaine and Lamia as representations of the female form in "Through the Looking Glass: Fairy-Tale Cinema and the Spectacle of Femininity in *Stardust* and *The Brothers Grimm*," *Marvels & Tales* 24, no. 1 (2010): 57–67.

10. Eshkeri, interviewed by author, 12 September 2012.

11. Although it is not so explicit in the film, in the novel of *Stardust* Una enchants Dunstan when she meets him in the prologue, and her knowledge of magic is significantly greater than that of her brothers.

12. I am grateful to Kate Daubney for pointing out the similarity between this aspect of Eshkeri's scoring strategy and the presence of "Tara's theme" in

Steiner's score to *Gone with the Wind* (1939), reaffirming the connection between Eshkeri's thematic approach, and practices developed during the studio era.

13. Paulus, "Williams versus Wagner or an Attempt at Linking Music Epics," 159.

14. Email from Ilan Eshkeri to Nick Ingman, date unknown. Made available by the composer.

15. Eshkeri, interviewed by author, 12 September 2012.

16. For connections between 'high art' music and criminality see, for instance, Thomas Fahy, "Killer Culture: Classical Music and the Art of Killing in *Silence of the Lambs* and *Se7en.*" *The Journal of Popular Culture* 37, no. 1 (2003): 28–42; Stan Link, "Sympathy with the devil? Music of the psycho post-*Psycho.*" *Screen* 45, no. 1 (2004): 1–20; David Ireland, "'It's a sin [. . .] using Ludwig van like that. He did no harm to anyone, Beethoven just wrote music': The role of the incongruent soundtrack in the representation of the cinematic criminal," in *Constructing Crime: Discourse and Cultural Representations of Crime and "Deviance,"* ed. C. Gregoriou (New York: Palgrave Macmillan, 2012), 97–111.

17. Kilar transcription by author.

18. Three parts of the melody for "Ruff *Stardust* Idea v3" are shown, since each section contributes to the final score. Similarly, "Tristan" is contracted in the web to present the sections that give rise to the "Royal Family" and "Tristan's Failure" leitmotifs.

19. Matt Brennan, "*Stardust*: Review," *Soundtracks.net* 2007, www.soundtrack.net/albums/database/?id=4585 (18 December 2012).

20. Clark Douglas, "*Stardust*—Ilan Eshkeri," *Movie Music UK* 2007, http://moviemusicuk.us/2007/08/10/stardust-ilan-eshkeri/ (18 December 2012). Original emphasis.

21. See, for instance, I.Q. Hunter, "Post-classical fantasy cinema: *The Lord of the Rings,*" in *The Cambridge Companion to Literature on Screen*, eds. Deborah Cartmell and Imelda Whelehan (Cambridge: Cambridge University Press, 2007), 154–66; Jim Smith and J. Clive Matthews, *The Lord of the Rings: The Films, The Books, The Radio Series* (London: Virgin Books, 2004). Janet K. Halfyard does touch on musical aspects of both films in "Introduction: Finding Fantasy," *The Music of Fantasy Cinema*, ed. Janet K. Halfyard (Sheffield: Equinox Publishing Ltd, 2012), 1–15.

22. Douglas's description could arguably be applied to a wide range of film-music genres since the establishment of the background score in the early 1930s.

23. See, for instance, Brennan, "*Stardust*: Review" (18 December 2012); Chris McEneany, "*Stardust*—Music from the Motion Picture Review," *AVForums* 2007, www.avforums.com/movies/index.php?showtitlereview=9151 (18 December 2012); "*Stardust,*" *Filmtracks: Modern Soundtrack Reviews* 2009, www.filmtracks.com/titles/stardust.html (18 December 2012). The labelling of all of Shore's themes is taken from Doug Adams, *The Music of The Lord of the Rings Films: A Comprehensive Account of Howard Shore's Scores* (Sri Lanka: Carpentier, 2010), 23.

24. Adams, *The Music of The Lord of the Rings Films*, 73.

25. Adams, *The Music of The Lord of the Rings Films*, 72–73.

26. Eshkeri's "Pirate" leitmotif is actually in $\frac{4}{4}$ with triplet quavers, but the resulting sound gives the impression of being in $\frac{12}{8}$.

27. W.S. Gilbert and Arthur Sullivan, *The Pirates of Penzance*, piano/vocal score (London: Chappell & Co., Ltd., [1879] N.D). The opening songs for the pirates are "Pour, oh pour, the pirate sherry" (pages 12–15) and "O better far to live and die," better known as the Pirate King's song (pages 18–20).

28. Personal communication with author, 10 February 2013.

29. Comments to this effect can be found in a number of the special features on the Blu-Ray release of the film. See *Stardust*, dir. Matthew Vaughn. Paramount Pictures, 2007 [Blu-Ray 2009].

30. Ssreverb, "What's That Song—Top Gear Season 10: [10x9] December 9th, 2007," *Final Gear* 2011, http://forums.finalgear.com/top-gear-episode-songs-season-10/10x9-december-9th-2007-a-23758/ (29 January 2013).

31. Ssreverb, "What's That Song—Top Gear Season 10: [10x10] December 23rd, 2007," *Final Gear* 2010, http://forums.finalgear.com/top-gear-episode-songs-season-10/10x10-december-23rd-2007-a-24063/ (29 January 2013). Lists of the music used in the BBC broadcasts of all episodes of *Top Gear* can be found at http://forums.finalgear.com/top-gear-episode-songs/.

APPENDIX

Credit list of those involved in the production of Eshkeri's *Stardust*.

Ilan Eshkeri—Composer

Eshkeri's Core Team

Andy Brown—Conductor; Music Contractor
Robert Elhai—Orchestrator
Vic Fraser—Music Preparation
Steve McLaughlin—Original Music Producer; Music Score Mixer
The London Metropolitan Orchestra—Music Performers

Music Production Team

Christoph Bauschinger—Music Production Assistant
John Finklea—Temp Music Editor
Liz Gallacher—Music Supervisor
Chad Hobson—Music Programmer
Natalie Holt—Music Production Assistant
Nick Ingman—Orchestrator
Jake Jackson—Music Scoring Recordist; Assistant Score Engineer
Daryl Kell—Music Editor
Julian Kershaw—Orchestrator
Elisa Kustow—Music Production Coordinator
Richard Lancaster—Music Score Mixer; Music Scoring Recordist
Marius Ruhland—Music Programmer
Scott Shields—Music Programmer
Jeff Toyne—Orchestrator

Film Production Team

Jon Harris—Editor
Tamsin Jeffrey—First Assistant Editor
Randy Spendlove—Executive Vice-President for Music and Creative Affairs (Paramount)
Matthew Vaughn—Director
James Winnifrith—Assistant Editor

BIBLIOGRAPHY

Adams, Doug. *The Music of* The Lord of the Rings *Films*. South Korea: Carpentier, 2010.

Adorno, Theodore, and Hans Eisler. *Composing for the Films*. 2nd edition. London: Continuum, [1947] 2005.

Allen, Michael. "From *Bwana Devil* to *Batman Forever*: Technology in Contemporary Hollywood Cinema." 109–29 in *Contemporary Hollywood Cinema*, edited by Steve Neale and Murray Smith. London: Routledge, 2004.

Barron, Lee. "'Music Inspired By...': The Curious Case of the Missing Soundtrack." 148–61 in *Popular Music and Film*, edited by Ian Inglis. London: Wallflower Press, 2003.

Barthes, Roland. "The Death of the Author." 142–48 in *Image–Music–Text*, edited and translated by Stephen Heath. New York: Hill, 1977.

Blair, Iain. "From the Bard to the Bean without missing a beat." *Variety*. 16 November 2011. www.variety.com/article/VR1118045841?refcatid=13 (16 October 2012).

Blanckley, Phil. "*Coriolanus*." *Static Mass Emporium: The Essence of Film*. 4 June 2012. http://staticmass.net/soundtracks/coriolanus-soundtrack-cd-2011-review/ (16 October 2012).

Brennan, Matt. "*Stardust*: Review." *Soundtracks.net*. 2007 www.soundtrack.net/albums/database/?id=4585 (18 December 2012).

Breznican, Anthony. "Storyteller Gaiman wishes upon a star: Movie magic touches his fairy tale *Stardust*," *USA Today*, 31 July 2007, 1D. Available online at http://usatoday30.usatoday.com/printedition/life/20070731/d_cover31.art.htm (30 November 2012).

Broadcasters' Audience Research Board. *BARB*. 2013. www.barb.co.uk (10 January 2013).

Buhler, James, Caryl Flinn, and David Neumeyer, eds. *Music and Cinema*.

Hanover, N.H.: Wesleyan University Press, 2000.

Burkholder, J. Peter. "Allusion," *Grove Music Online. Oxford Music Online.* 2012.   http://0-www.oxfordmusiconline.com.wam.leeds.ac.uk/ subscriber/article/grove/music/52852 (27 November 2012).

————. "Quotation," *Grove Music Online. Oxford Music Online.* 2012. http://0-www.oxfordmusiconline.com.wam.leeds.ac.uk/subscriber/ article/grove/music/52854 (27 November 2012).

Burt, George. *The Art of Film Music: Special Emphasis on Hugo Friedhofer, Alex North, David Raksin, Leonard Rosenman.* Boston, Mass: Northeastern University Press, 1994.

Cahill, Susan. "Through the Looking Glass: Fairy-Tale Cinema and the Spectacle of Femininity in *Stardust* and *The Brothers Grimm.*" *Marvels & Tales* 24, no. 1 (2010): 57–67.

Capone. "Capone talks to Matthew Vaughn about *Stardust*, Bobby De Niro, *X-Men*, *Thor* and much more!!!" *Aint it Cool News.* 2007. www.aintitcool.com/node/33607 (30 November 2012).

Carlin Sr., Dan. *Music in Film and Video Productions.* London: Focal Press, 1991.

Carlsson, Mikael. "Mr Kamen's Final Opus: An interview with Steve McLaughlin, Christopher Brooks and Robert Elhai." Liner notes to Michael Kamen. *Back to Gaya: Original Motion Picture Soundtrack.* Sweden: Moviescore Media, 2012 [CD].

Carnevale, Rob. "*Stardust*—Matthew Vaughn and Neil Gaiman interview." *IndieLondon.*   n.d.   www.indielondon.co.uk/Film-Review/stardust- matthew-vaughn-and-neil-gaiman-interview (30 November 2012).

Cartmell, Deborah. "Text to Screen: Introduction." 23–28 in *Adaptations: From Text to Screen, Screen to Text*, edited by Deborah Cartmell and Imelda Whelehan. New York: Routledge, 1999.

Cooke, Mervyn. *A History of Film Music.* Cambridge: Cambridge University Press, 2008.

Cooper, David. *Bernard Herrmann's* The Ghost and Mrs. Muir: *A Film Score Guide.* Lanham, Md.: Scarecrow Press, 2005.

Cooper, David, Christopher Fox and Ian Sapiro, eds. "Keynote Interview with Trevor Jones." 1–14 in *CineMusic? Constructing the Film Score*, edited by David Cooper, Christopher Fox and Ian Sapiro. Newcastle- upon-Tyne: Cambridge Scholars Publishing, 2008.

Curry, Alice. "'The pale trees shook, although no wind blew, and it seemed to Tristran that they shook in anger': 'blind space' and ecofeminism in a post-colonial reading of Neil Gaiman and Charles Vess's graphic novel *Stardust* (1998)." *Barnboken—Journal of Children's Literature Research* 33, no. 2 (2010): 19–33.

Daubney, Kate. *Max Steiner's* Now, Voyager: *A Film Score Guide.* Westport, Conn.: Greenwood Press, 2000.

Davis, Richard. *Complete Guide to Film Scoring: The Art and Business of Writing Music for Movies and TV*. Boston, Mass.: Berklee Press, 1999.

Donnelly, K.J., ed. *Film Music: Critical Approaches*. Edinburgh: Edinburgh University Press, 2001.

Douglas, Clark. "*Stardust*—Ilan Eshkeri." *Movie Music UK*. 2007. http://moviemusicuk.us/2007/08/10/stardust-ilan-eshkeri/ (18 December 2012).

Douglas, Edward. "Interview with Matthew Vaughn." *SuperHeroHype*. 2007. www.superherohype.com/features/articles/94533-exclusive-stardust-director-matthew-vaughn (9 November 2012).

Dvořák, Antonín. *Slavonic Dances* Op. 46. Prague: Státní nakladatelství krásné literatury, [1878] 1955.

Eshkeri, Ilan. *Centurion: Original Soundtrack*. Sweden: Moviescore Media, 2010 [CD].

———. "*Coriolanus*—Ilan Eshkeri Composer Interview." *YouTube.com*. 24 February 2012. www.youtube.com/watch?v=MH5vK4BjCsQ&feature=plcp (16 October 2012).

———. *Johnny English Reborn*. Los Angeles. Varese Sarabande/Colosseum Music. 2011 [CD].

———. *Ninja Assassin: Original Soundtrack*. New York. Sony, 2010 [CD].

———. *The Young Victoria*. London. EMI. 2009 [CD].

Fahy, Thomas. "Killer Culture: Classical Music and the Art of Killing in *Silence of the Lambs* and *Se7en*." *The Journal of Popular Culture* 37, no. 1 (2003): 28–42.

Fleming, Michael. "Starry cast for *Stardust*: Thesps align for Vaughn-helmed Gaiman adaptation." *Variety*. 2006. www.variety.com/article/VR1117939318 (30 November 2012).

Flood, Alison. "Neil Gaiman wins Carnegie Medal." *Guardian.co.uk*. 24 June 2010. www.guardian.co.uk/books/2010/jun/24/neil-gaiman-carnegie-graveyard-book (30 November 2012).

Foucault, Michael "What is an Author?" 101–20 in *The Foucault Reader: An Introduction to Foucault's Thought*, edited by Paul Rabinow. London: Penguin Books, 1984.

Gaiman, Neil. *Stardust*. London: Headline Publishing Group, 1999.

Gentry, Ric, and Dede Allen. "An Interview with Dede Allen." *Film Quarterly* 46, no. 1 (Autumn 1992): 12–22.

Gilbert, W.S., and Arthur Sullivan. *The Pirates of Penzance*. Piano/vocal score. London: Chappell & Co., Ltd., [1879] N.D.

Gorbman, Claudia. *Unheard Melodies: Narrative Film Music*. Bloomington, Ind.: Indiana University Press, 1987.

Hagen, Earle. *Scoring for Films*. Updated edition. Los Angeles: Alfred Publishing Co., Inc., 1971.

Halfyard, Janet. *Danny Elfman's* Batman: A Film Score Guide. Lanham, Md.:

Scarecrow Press, 2004.

———., ed. *The Music of Fantasy Cinema*. Sheffield: Equinox Publishing Ltd, 2012.

Hiscock, John. "Matthew Vaughn: The Brit who's making the stars shine." *The Telegraph*. 5 October 2007. www.telegraph.co.uk/culture/film/starsandstories/3668336/Matthew-Vaughn-The-Brit-whos-making-the-stars-shine.html (30 November 2012).

Holsen, Laura M. and Sharon Waxman. "A Shuffle at Paramount and more to come." *New York Times*. 11 January 2007. www.nytimes.com/2007/01/11/business/media/11studio.html?scp=1&sq=paramount&st=nyt&_r=0 (5 December 2012).

———. "Turmoil continues at Paramount Pictures as president resigns." *New York Times*. 11 January 2007. http://www.nytimes.com/2007/01/11/technology/11iht-studio.4169382.html (5 December 2012).

Hunter, I.Q. "Post-classical fantasy cinema: *The Lord of the Rings*." 154–66 in *The Cambridge Companion to Literature on Screen*, edited by Deborah Cartmell and Imelda Whelehan. Cambridge: Cambridge University Press, 2007.

Hurwitz, Matt. "Scoring for Picture: Hans Zimmer's Scoring Collective—Composer Collaboration at Remote Control Productions." 254–7 in *The Routledge Film Music Source Book*, edited by James Wierzbicki, Nathan Platte and Colin Roust. New York: Routledge, [2007] 2012.

Hutcheon, Linda. *A Theory of Adaptation*. New York: Routledge, 2006.

Inglis, Ian, ed. *Popular Music and Film*. London: Wallflower Press, 2003.

Ireland, David. "'It's a sin [. . .] using Ludwig van like that. He did no harm to anyone, Beethoven just wrote music': The role of the incongruent soundtrack in the representation of the cinematic criminal." 97–111 in *Constructing Crime: Discourse and Cultural Representations of Crime and "Deviance,"* edited by C. Gregoriou. New York: Palgrave Macmillan, 2012.

John-Steiner, Vera. *Creative Collaboration*. Oxford: Oxford University Press, 2000.

Jones, Stephen. *Stardust: The Visual Companion*. London: Titan Books, 2007.

Kalinak, Kathryn. *Settling the Score: Music and the Classic Hollywood Film*. Madison: University of Wisconsin Press, 1992.

Karlin, Fred, and Rayburn Wright. *On the Track: A Guide to Contemporary Film Scoring*. Revised 2nd edition. New York: Routledge, 2004.

Kassabian, Anahid. *Hearing Film: Tracking Identifications in Contemporary Hollywood Film Music*. New York: Routledge, 2001.

Kompanek, Sonny. *From Score to Screen: Sequencers, Scores and Second Thoughts: The New Film Scoring Process*. New York: Schirmer Trade Books, 2004.

Leader, Michael. "Matthew Vaughn interview: *X-Men: First Class, Thor*,

Hollywood, James Bond, Take That and more." *Den of Geek*. 2011. www.denofgeek.com/movies/james-bond/17507/matthew-vaughn-interview-x-men-first-class-thor-hollywood-james-bond-take-that-and-more (30 November 2012).

Levy, Emanuel. "Interviews: Stardust with Matthew Vaughn." *Emanuel Levy*. n.d. www.emanuellevy.com/interview/stardust-with-matthew-vaughn-2/ (30 November 2012).

Linder, Christopher, ed. *The James Bond Phenomenon: A Critical Reader*. Manchester: Manchester University Press, 2003.

Link, Stan. "Sympathy with the devil? Music of the psycho post-*Psycho*." *Screen* 45, no. 1 (2004): 1–20.

LoBrutto, Vincent. *Sound-on-Film: Interviews with Creators of Film Sound*. Westport, Conn.: Praeger Publishers, 1994.

MacDonald, Laurence E. *The Invisible Art of Film Music: A Comprehensive History*. New York: Ardsley House Publishers, Inc., 1998.

Mansell, John. "Interview with Ilan Eshkeri." *Soundtrack: The Cinemascore and Soundtrack Archives*. 2011. www.runmovies.eu (15 Aug. 2012).

McFarlane, Brian. "Reading Film and Literature." 15–28 in *The Cambridge Companion to Literary Adaptation*, edited by Deborah Cartmell and Imelda Whelehan. Cambridge: Cambridge University Press, 2007.

McNary, Dave, and Nicole Laporte. "Par sprinkles *Stardust*: Vaughn to adapt, helm Gaiman novel." *Variety*. 2005. www.variety.com/article/VR1117931609 (30 November 2012).

Mera, Miguel. *Mychael Danna's* The Ice Storm: *A Film Score Guide*. Lanham, Md.: Scarecrow Press, 2007.

Moriarty. "Moriarty Visits London For A Dash Of *Stardust*! Part One Of Two!!" *Aint it Cool News*. 21 July 2006. www.aintitcool.com/node/23933 (8 January 2013).

MTV. "*Stardust* Author Neil Gaiman Tells Why He Turns Down Most Adaptations—But Not This One." *MTV*. 2007. www.mtv.com/news/articles/1566862/neil-gaiman-makes-his-stardust.jhtml (30 November 2012).

Mythopoeic Society. "Mythopoeic Awards: Winners." *Mythopoeic Society*. 2012. www.mythsoc.org/awards/winners/ (30 November 2012).

Offenbach, Jacques. *Orphée aux Enfers*. Berlin: Bote & Bock, [1858] 1999.

"Open Range." *Filmtracks: Modern Soundtrack Reviews*. 2003, rev. 2009. www.filmtracks.com/titles/open_range.html (4 Apr. 2012).

Paget, Derek. "Speaking Out: The Transformations of *Trainspotting*." 128–40 in *Adaptations: From Text to Screen, Screen to Text*, edited by Deborah Cartmell and Imelda Whelehan. New York: Routledge, 1999.

Paulus, Irena. "Williams versus Wagner or an Attempt at Linking Music Epics." *International Review of the Aesthetics and Sociology of Music* 31, no. 2 (2000): 153–84.

Quint. "Quint wanders around Pinewood and checks out Matthew Vaughn's *Stardust*!!!" *Aint it Cool News*. 7 July 2006. www.aintitcool. com/node/23785 (8 January 2013).

R, Chuck. "Episode 53." Podcast. *Krypton Fan*. 2006. http://chuckr7. hipcast.com/deluge/3adea8c1-5dd3-38cf-3dba-9df262e2f06e.mp3 (8 January 2013).

Rona, Jeff. *The Reel World, Scoring for Pictures; A Practical Guide to the Art, Technology and Business of Composing for Film and Television*. San Francisco: Miller Freeman Books, 2000.

Rusnak, Marcin. "Blessings and curses of the silver screen: Film adaptations of *Coraline* and *Stardust* by Neil Gaiman." 139–49 in *Alternate Life-Worlds in Literary Fiction*, edited by Ewa Kębłowska-Ławniczak, Zdzisław Wąsik and Teresa Bruś. Wrocław: Wyższa Szkoła Filologiczna we Wrocławiu, 2011.

Sadoff, Ron. "The role of the music editor and the 'temp track' as blueprint for the score, source music, and scource music of films." *Popular Music* 25, no. 2 (2006): 165–83.

Said, Edward W. *Orientalism*. London: Routledge and Kegan Paul, 1978.

Sapiro, Ian. Scoring the Score: The Role of the Orchestrator in the Contemporary British Film Industry. Diss., University of Leeds, 2011.

Scorenotes. "Interview with Ilan Eshkeri." *ScoreNotes*. 2007. http://scorenotes.com/interview/eshkeri/ilan_eshkeri.html (15 August 2012).

Shearmur, Edward. *Johnny English: Original Motion Picture Soundtrack*. Universal Classics. 2003 [CD].

Smith, Jeff. *The Sounds of Commerce: Marketing Popular Film Music*. New York: Columbia University Press, 1998.

Smith, Jim, and J. Clive Matthews. *The Lord of the Rings: The Films, The Books, The Radio Series*. London: Virgin Books, 2004.

"*Stardust*." *Filmtracks: Modern Soundtrack Reviews*. 2009. www.filmtracks. com/titles/stardust.html (18 December 2012).

Sutcliffe, Phil. "Instrumental to the Film." *Leeds Alumni Magazine* 11 (Summer 2012): 14–17.

Swain, Joseph P. *The Broadway Musical: A Critical and Musical Survey*. New York: Oxford University Press, 1990.

"*The Young Victoria*: Production Notes." GK Films, LLC, 2008.

"Trailer Music." *SoundTrack.Net*. 2013. www.soundtrack.net/trailers/ (11 January 2013).

Van Wassenhove, Marie-Lise. "Interview with Ilan Eshkeri." *Filmmuziek.be*. 2004. www.filmmuziek.be (15 Aug. 2012).

Various artists. *Layer Cake*. London. EMI. 2005 [CD].

Walker, Alan, Maria Eckhardt, and Rena Charnin Mueller. "Liszt, Franz," *Grove Music Online. Oxford Music Online*. 2012. http://0-

www.oxfordmusiconline.com.wam.leeds.ac.uk/subscriber/article/gro ve/music/48265pg28 (26 November 2012).

Wampler, Angela. "*Stardust* — 'It's *Pirates Of The Caribbean* Meets *The Princess Bride.*'" *A! Magazine for the Arts.* 29 May 2007. http://artsmagazine.info/articles.php?view=detail&id=07052920161 174501 (8 January 2013).

"What's That Song—*Top Gear.*" *Final Gear.* 2013. http://forums.finalgear. com/top-gear-episode-songs (29 January 2013).

Whittall, Arnold. "Leitmotif," *Grove Music Online. Oxford Music Online.* 2012. http://0-www.oxfordmusiconline.com.wam.leeds.ac.uk/sub scriber/article/grove/music/16360 (21 November 2012).

Winters, Benjamin. *Erich Wolfgang Korngold's* The Adventures of Robin Hood: *A Film Score Guide.* Lanham, Md.: Scarecrow Press, 2007.

World Fantasy Board. "1991 World Fantasy Award Winners and Nominees." *World Fantasy Convention.* 1991. www.worldfantasy.org/awards/ 1991.html (7 December 2012).

Wrobel, Bill. "Self-Borrowing in the Music of Bernard Herrmann." *Journal of Film Music* 2 (2003): 249–71.

Young Library Adult Services Association. "Alex Awards—2000 Selection(s)." *American Literary Association.* 2000. www.ala.org/ awardsgrants/awards/231/winners/2000 (30 November 2012).

Other Resources

Colosseum: A Gladiator's Story. Dir. Tilman Remme. BBC Video. 2003 [DVD].

Hannibal Rising. Dir. Peter Webber. Young Hannibal Productions. 2007 [DVD].

Internet Movie Database. www.imdb.com.

Ring of the Nibelungs. Dir. Uli Edel. Tandem Communications. 2004 [DVD].

Stardust. Dir. Matthew Vaughn. Paramount Pictures. 2007 [Blu-ray 2009].

The Snowman and the Snowdog. Dir. Hilary Audus. Snowman Enterprises. 2012 [Television Program].

INDEX

Zimmer, Hans, 3, 6–7, 12, 16, 125; *Black Hawk Down*, 6; *Gladiator*, 12; Remote Control, 6, 16; *The Peacemaker*, 3

ABOUT THE AUTHOR

Ian Sapiro is Lecturer in Music at the University of Leeds. His research interests include film music, particularly the processes of film-score production, musical theatre, orchestration, and the crossovers between them. He is author of "The Filmmaker's Contract: Controlling Sonic Space in the Films of Peter Greenaway" in *Music, Sound and Filmmakers: Sonic Style in Cinema* (edited by James Wierzbicki, Routledge, 2012) and coauthor of "A Source-Studies Approach to Michael Nyman's Score for *The Draughtsman's Contract*" (*Journal of Film Music* 3, no. 2, Spring 2011: 155–70).